DEPART FROM ME

The Dreadful Words of Jesus Christ to Many

A THEOLOGICAL ASSESSMENT OF AMERICAN CHRISTIANITY

Reginald F. Davis, Ph.D.

an imprint of Sunbury Press, Inc.
Mechanicsburg, PA USA

an imprint of Sunbury Press, Inc.
Mechanicsburg, PA USA

Copyright © 2025 by Reginald F. Davis.
Cover Copyright © 2025 by Sunbury Press, Inc.

Sunbury Press supports copyright. Copyright fuels creativity, encourages diverse voices, promotes free speech, and creates a vibrant culture. Thank you for buying an authorized edition of this book and for complying with copyright laws by not reproducing, scanning, or distributing any part of it in any form without permission. You are supporting writers and allowing Sunbury Press to continue to publish books for every reader. For information contact Sunbury Press, Inc., Subsidiary Rights Dept., PO Box 548, Boiling Springs, PA 17007 USA or legal@sunburypress.com.

For information about special discounts for bulk purchases, please contact Sunbury Press Orders Dept. at (855) 338-8359 or orders@sunburypress.com.

To request one of our authors for speaking engagements or book signings, please contact Sunbury Press Publicity Dept. at publicity@sunburypress.com.

FIRST SCRIPTORIA PRESS EDITION: May 2025

Set in Adobe Garamond | Interior design by Crystal Devine | Cover by Lawrence Knorr | Edited by Lawrence Knorr.

Publisher's Cataloging-in-Publication Data
Names: Davis, Reginald F., author.
Title: Depart from me the dreadful words of Jesus Christ to many : a theological assessment of American Christianity / Reginald F. Davis, Ph.D.
Description: First trade paperback edition. | Mechanicsburg, PA : Scriptoria Press, 2025.
Summary: The goal of this book is to encourage American Christians to examine and loose themselves from the traditions, mythologies, and ideologies of injustice under the guise of Christianity, and join Christ in the transformation of the American Empire and the world. American Christianity needs a provoking and shaking to forsake the error of their ways to avoid hearing the dreadful words of Jesus Christ, "Depart From Me!"
Identifiers: ISBN 979-8-88819-311-2 (softcover).
Subjects: RELIGION / Biblical Studies / New Testament / Jesus, the Gospels & Acts | RELIGION / Christian Living / Personal Growth.| RELIGION / Christianity / Baptist.

Designed in the USA
0 1 1 2 3 5 8 13 21 34 55

For the Love of Books!

To all Christians who believe that Jesus Christ is Lord!

CONTENTS

Acknowledgments   vii
Introduction   1

CHAPTERS

1	Everybody Talking About Heaven Is Not Going There	11
2	Heaven Is For Prepared People	29
3	Unfaithful Steward	41
4	Banned From the Banquet	54
5	Neglect Brings Eternal Regret	64
6	Fruitless Christians	74
7	Traveling the Wrong Road	82
8	Lukewarm Christians	95
9	Cultural Christians	108
10	Thermometer Christians	123

Conclusion   133
Bibliography   142
About the Author   148

ACKNOWLEDGMENTS

I would like to acknowledge my wife, Myrlene, and family for their encouragement and support. I want to thank Lawrence Knorr and the Sunbury Press for their kindness, professionalism, and support in publishing this work.

INTRODUCTION

Therefore, do not deceive yourself! Of all deceivers, fear most yourself!" —Søren Kierkegaard

There has been an expectation for over two millenniums of the imminent return of Jesus Christ. Events happening in real-time across the world, many believe, point to the soon return of the King of Glory. How close we are to Christ's return, nobody really knows. But, what we do know is eventually, Christology, eschatology, ecclesiology, and anthropology are to come together finally in one single event called Judgment Day. In other words, every Christian and non-Christian shall one day stand before the judgment seat of Christ for final salvation or damnation. Everybody I know wants to go to heaven. Every pastor and congregation wants to go to heaven. Every parent, friend, colleague, and Christian educator from every nation and tongue wants to enter the Kingdom of God. But, the desire and destination of many won't match. According to Jesus Christ, who is the Author and Finisher of our faith, many will hear the dreadful words, "Depart from Me." Those who hear these words are dreadfully and shamefully lost forever. Their souls are eternally separated from the Savior without any possible recourse. The word Christian is used because it conveys followers of Jesus Christ, but these dreadful words of Jesus Christ are not exclusive to Christians but to many people, irrespective of their religious persuasion. In fact, when Jesus spoke these words, "Depart from Me," He didn't specify any religion or denomination. He didn't say, "Depart from me Hindu, Buddha, Judah, Muslim, Christian, Catholic, Protestant, Lutheran, Baptist,

Methodist, Presbyterian, non denomination, etc. Jesus said, "Many shall say to Me in that day, 'Lord, Lord, have we not prophesied in Your name, cast out demons in Your name, and done many wonders in Your name? And then I will declare to them, 'I never knew you; depart from Me, you who practice lawlessness (Matthew 7:21-23)!"

Understand (many) represents all religions, including those who call themselves Christians. For the purposes of this book, American Christianity is the focus of our theological assessment, and it represents predominantly white catholic and evangelical Christians who are the dominant racial and religious groups and who hold most of the power and wealth in the country. Although the percentage is small, American Christianity also includes other racial groups. Based upon research, American catholic and evangelical Christianity is the dominant practice of this land instead of the Christianity of Christ. Many, not all, will be surprised and feel Soren Kierkegaard's sickening dread to hear these words of Jesus Christ: "Depart from Me." Leaders and people who thought they were sure to make heaven because they had such a big and growing ministry will be surprised. Churches, big and small, that were on many corners in communities will be surprised they won't enter into the Kingdom of God. Leaders we considered icons in the ministry will be surprised. People who were gifted in preaching, teaching, singing, administration, building, and counseling will be surprised at the words of Jesus Christ. The point is the size of the ministry, the reputation of the person, or the amazing gift people possessed while on earth have nothing to do with why Jesus will speak these words to many. These words will be spoken to many because their vertical faith was out of alignment with their horizontal practice. There was a lot of religious orthodoxy but little to no orthopraxy. There was a lot of lip service, but hearts were far from the Lord. There was too much religion, very little humanity, and the unwillingness to repent while tolerating social and economic structures of injustice that are destructive to the poor and oppressed is one of the major reasons many won't make it into the Kingdom of God. When Jesus says, "You who practice lawlessness," He is speaking in terms of an unjust system that rewards one race and punishes another; a system that creates wealth, power, and privilege for one group while at the same time creating poverty, injustice, and inequality for other groups. Those who protest and defend such a system are participating in its lawlessness. Many who preach piety from the pulpit but never call out perpetrators of injustice and inequality will be surprised at the condemnation of the words of Jesus. People who thought they were being good American Christians while being complicit overtly or covertly in the practices of racism and oppression will be stunned to hear "Depart from Me."

The glitter that looked like gold will be exposed this day. The wolf that was covered in sheep's clothing will be made known. The preacher who prophesied in Jesus's name will be shown to be a liar. The hirelings who made merchandise of the people of God, the covering will be pulled off this day. Those who thought they were getting by with their economic schemes, strategies, undercover deals, and corruption will find out they didn't escape God's judgment. The scale of people and nations will be weighed in the balance, and many will be found wanting and, therefore, condemned to utter darkness. Money, power, position, title, class privilege, and political party won't vindicate this day. The loopholes used to get out of moral responsibility won't work this day. The mythologies and ideologies used to obfuscate the deep-rooted hatred and disdainment of poor and oppressed people will be blown wide open for divine retribution. "There will be weeping and gnashing of teeth (Matthew 13:42)."

I write this book with a sense of urgency, hoping that those who read it will get in a hurry, repent, and do God's Will before it is too late. All of us need to do some self-examination to make sure we are authentically doing the Will of God and not our own. American Christianity that gives rise to the division in the church and nation must turn from its wrongdoing before the cord of life is cut. Divine retribution is coming, and hopefully, this book gives us time to reflect, assess, pray, and move us to repentance. It is past time for American Christianity to straighten up and fly right. It is not enough to get people saved; this is only a start. Salvation includes not only the "here after" but also the "here and now." The Kingdom of God is the will of God on earth as it is in heaven. To substitute one for the other is not the Christianity of Christ. American Christianity is too preoccupied with the bliss of heaven and not enough concern for correcting the hell on earth. If the earth is not worth the time to transform, then it was not worth the time for Jesus coming to earth. But, since Jesus did come and bring us the Kingdom of God, those who claim to be His followers must be engaged in the same work of the Kingdom. This work is not to defend and depend on an unjust system but to transform it into the Kingdom of God. Anything less than this is not enough to gain access to the Kingdom of God. It is possible to be close to the Kingdom of God and not enter into it. Charles Spurgeon said, "Almost saved is altogether lost! There are many in Hell who once were almost saved but who are now altogether damned. Think of that: you are not far from the Kingdom. It is being in the Kingdom that saves the soul, not being near the Kingdom."[1]

If this book doesn't describe your life and ministry, wonderful; keep letting your light shine and truthfully doing the Will of God. However, oftentimes, when we think a message is not for us—it is directly pointing to us. When we point a finger at others, three fingers are pointing back at us. In short, we could be the very ones this book is speaking to. We all have blind spots and are ignorant of many of the sins of which we are guilty. Therefore, before you dismiss this book for someone else, read it for yourself, and in it, you may think you are saved and could be far from it. You may think you are a disciple of Christ but come to realize you are really not. You may think you are serving the God of Jesus Christ, but maybe worshipping an idol god instead. Should this book unhinge you, the Holy Spirit is working to motivate you to repent from the "Sin that so easily entangles (Hebrews 12:1)." American Christianity needs to repent from the sin of racism and oppression. If nothing else, I hope this book raises consciousness about the consequences of our actions as we stand before a just and righteous Judge. The goal is to get us to examine ourselves to see if we are of the faith. "Unless, of course, [we] fail the test (2 Corinthians 13:5)." If we fail the test, at least we know we have work to do to get our houses in order before it is too late. It is unforgivable to have failed the faith test and find out later when it is too late. It will be disappointing to think we have eternal life and find out later we don't. There will be inordinate dread to know that out of all the people who were fooled and deceived on earth, these same people will see those who did the fooling and deceiving denounced from entering into the Kingdom of God.

---

1. Charles Spurgeon, "Almost Isn't Good Enough," www.spurgeongems.org

Therefore, this book is a wake-up call to American Christianity. Much of the problem lies with Christians who are too quiet and uninvolved in bringing to bear the full weight of their influence on the socioeconomic and political life of the nation. Unless the church dislodges injustice among its ranks, it stands in danger of hearing the words of the Savior, "Depart From Me!" Using some of the parables of Jesus, this project aims to help the church see itself as complicit in the ongoing injustice and inequality of God's people. To get rid of the nation's original sin, it takes the whole church—white and black—to eliminate it. The church cannot endorse the American Empire of injustice and the Kingdom of God at the same time. The church must choose where its allegiance lies.

I hope that this book opens the eyes of many so they can loose themselves from the traditions, mythologies and ideologies of injustice under the guise of Christianity and join Christ in the transformation of the American Empire and the world. This book is a necessary measuring rod to see how far off the church is from the faith and life of Jesus Christ and what the church must do to measure up to the standards of His Kingdom. Those who are ministering in Jesus' name and have no concern for social and economic justice while prostituting the gospel for power and material gain should read this book, repent, and truthfully call on the Savior now before it is too late. Only through repentance will Jesus Christ take people's feet off the crooked avenue and put them on the straight street. This book does not judge who is saved and who is not saved. No one really knows this but the Savior. This book is only a critique of the practices of people who consider themselves Christians in comparison with the Gospel of Jesus Christ and the prophets. For intent and purposes, this book is for all our consideration, and if the shoe fits, acknowledge it, repent, and then join Jesus Christ in demonstrating God's reign in human history. Many people think they are saved because they believe in God, go to church, and attend mass. These are indicators of being a religious practitioner but do not necessarily mean one has a living relationship with the Son of God. Remember, the Pharisees thought the same and worked against the Son of God. Jesus said, "Search the scriptures, for in them you think you have eternal life (John 5:39)."

Religious practice doesn't guarantee salvation any more than being close to the Kingdom of God. For there are many religious practitioners who oppress, murder, rape, and destroy people. Just investigate how American Christianity supported the violence of slavery and today's transgenerational oppression. Being religious can and does often work against the Kingdom of God. Also, the giving of time, talent, and treasure is not a green light to enter into the Kingdom of God. We cannot buy Christ's salvation or do anything to merit it. Salvation is a gift that must be accepted not on our terms but on God's terms through Christ.

Remember Simon the sorcerer! He thought he could buy the Holy Spirit and use it for selfish gain. He thought it was some kind of magic that he could manipulate to practice his old sorcery in a new way. But Peter told Simon, "May your money perish with you because you thought you could buy the gift of God with money! You have no part or share in this ministry because your heart is not right before God. Repent of this wickedness and pray to the Lord in the hope that he may forgive you for having such a thought in your heart. For I see that you are full of bitterness and captive to sin (Acts 8:20-23)." There are still Simons' in the pulpit, in the pew, and in some form of public and private ministry. Unless people truly repent of their transgressions, be they individual or collective, that are causing pain, suffering, death, grief, injustice, and outright division in the nation and the world, they are sure to hear the dreadful words of the Savior, "Depart from Me."

Since Christ has not yet appeared, the church has an opportunity to repent from the personal, religious, economic, social, political, and reprehensible things that could cause us to hear the dreadful words of Jesus Christ. Hopefully, we take this opportunity and come to repentance. Saul was convicted and repented and became Paul. Conviction is good; it helps us to take a deeper look at ourselves and turn away from practices that will have dreadful consequences. Giving Christ our hearts and minds may cause great loss on earth but it is well worth it when we hear Christ say, "Well Done!" Our concern should not be what people think of us but what Jesus Christ knows of us. I sincerely hope and pray that this book cuts to the hearts of leaders and people like Peter's sermon did on the Day of Pentecost that motivated people to ask, "What must we do to be saved." Then, we can simply say, as Peter said, "Repent and be baptized, every one of you, in the name of Jesus Christ for the forgiveness of your sins. And you will receive the gift of the Holy Spirit. The promise is for you and your children and for all who are far off—for all whom the Lord our God will call (Acts 2:38)." This act of repentance and the receiving of the Holy Spirit is not a one-time event, and its back to business as usual. If this is the case, then the process people went through was a cultural, religious rite, an expectation of the family, church, and community, but not a spiritual rebirth that produces a relationship with Jesus Christ.

The cultural ritual of repentance creates the delusion people are saved by admiring Christ but not truly following Christ. Sadly, this is the case with many people who call themselves Christians. "If a faith is only culturally inherited without a response to the saving work of Christ, that legacy, which should be a blessing, can become a barrier. In cultural Christianity, it is common for one to see himself as being born into Christianity rather than actually being born again."[2] This is the reason Jesus said, "They will put you out of the synagogues; yes, the time is coming that whoever kills you will think that he offers God service (John 16:2)." Who doubts America's historical record of racism, slavery and oppression, while claiming to be a Christian nation? Who doubts that racism is still a problem in American Christianity and that it causes division in the Body of Christ which "The races confess the same creeds, engage in the same forms of worship, nurture the same hopes, but do so in divided churches, where white and black find it easier to confess than to practice their common sonship to God."[3] Did not Jesus say, "You will know them by their fruits (Matthew 7:16)." Since some churches are complicit in their silence against racial injustice and serving as a cover for the socioeconomic structures in society, doesn't this say the church is part of the same tree that produces the bad fruit?

Notwithstanding, the black church, too, must move from its business-as-usual posture and develop more liberating rather than survival models of existence. The revolutionary Spirit Christ has given the black church throughout its tenure must be recaptured. The black church has struggled vigorously against racism, injustice, and inequality, but over time, it has allowed the fire of its resistance to be reduced to a flicker. The

---

2. Dean Inserra, *The Unsaved Christian Reaching Cultural Christianity with the Gospel* (Chicago: Moody Publishers, 2019), 59–60.
3. H. Richard Niebuhr, *The Social Sources of Denominationalism*, (New York: World Publishing Company, 1929), 11.

transformation of structural injustice cannot happen unless there is a radical break from these unjust social structures to reshape society. As long as the black church and communities they serve continue their participation in unjust structures, a new society can never spring forth. Serving Christ and taking favors from unjust social structures of oppression puts the black church in a morally neutral position to only later be dismissed by Christ Himself. This is to say both the white and black churches must repent before it is too late.

The mission of American Christianity is to proclaim and work for the reign of the Kingdom of God on earth and not some ideology and political party that creates conditions of poverty and injustice. Being silent and allowing socioeconomic injustice and inequality to continue makes American Christianity just as guilty as the builders of the unjust structures. Paul Tillich said, "It is never the nation which is directly guilty for what is done by the nation. It is always the ruling group. But, all individuals in a nation are responsible for the existence of the ruling group. Not many individuals in Germany are directly guilty of Nazi atrocities. But all of them are responsible for the acceptance of a government which was willing and able to do such things."[4]

Until American Christianity realizes that it is in spiritual error and operating outside the Will of God and repents, many will not enter the Kingdom of God. Too many people think all they have to do is appeal for the grace of God, and all is well. Grace is given as an opportunity to repent not as a license to continue the practice of business as usual. Continuing business as usual while claiming grace is what Dietrich Bonhoeffer called cheap grace. "Cheap grace is the grace we bestow on ourselves. Cheap grace is the preaching of forgiveness without requiring repentance, baptism without church discipline, Communion without confession . . . Cheap grace is grace without discipleship, grace without the cross, grace without Jesus Christ, living and incarnate."[5] True repentance is required to enter into the Kingdom of God. American Christianity must give up its racial prejudice, its complicity in racism, and its covenant with the enemy of our souls if they expect to enter into the Kingdom of God. We cannot enter by

---

4. Paul Tillich, "*Love, Power, and Justice*" *Christian Social Teaching*, complied by George W. Corelli (Minneapolis, MN: Augsburg Publishing House, 1966), 408.

5. Dietrich Bonhoeffer, *The Cost of Discipleship*, Macmillan Paper Back Edition, 1979, 47.

anything else other than by having a relationship with God through Jesus Christ. Neutrality won't be acceptable at the judgment seat of Jesus Christ. Dante Alighieri reminds us, "The darkest places in hell are reserved for those who maintained their neutrality in times of moral crisis."[6] We must choose whom we will serve, and this choice determines words of commendation or condemnation spoken to us by Jesus Christ the Lord! Again, this book is a measuring rod for us to see our shortcomings and repent. Paul said, "For if we would judge ourselves, we would not be judged. But when we are judged, we are chastened by the Lord, that we may not be condemned with the world (1 Corinthians 11:31-32)."

The following chapters are biblical reasons many people may hear "Depart from Me." Based upon the parables of Jesus and other biblical sayings, these chapters are written to help wake up American Christianity to be the church Jesus Christ is calling it to be. If American Christianity refuses the call to repent, then all hope is lost. Once the verdict is pronounced, it is final. There is no appellate court of appeals. There is no lower tribunal to overturn the decision because of a technicality. No coup can overturn the Lord's decision. Jesus Christ is the Judge, the Jury, and the Executioner of our souls. Therefore, brothers and sisters, I beseech you not to be among those who will hear the dreadful words of Jesus Christ, "Depart From Me!"

---

6. Dante Alighieri, *Divine Comedy* (Everyman's Library, Publisher, 1995).

Chapter One

EVERYBODY TALKING ABOUT HEAVEN IS NOT GOING THERE

Aim at heaven, and you will get earth thrown in. Aim at earth, and you get neither. —CS. Lewis

All of my life, I have been hearing about people desiring to go to heaven. As the son of a pastor, the church was the life of the family and community. Every week, and sometimes two or three times a week, church service was centered on going to heaven. Sermons and songs were about going to heaven. It gave people split moments of transcendence to forget the harsh realities of this life. The overall thrust of the black church was a preoccupation with going to heaven and a deemphasis on transforming the world. Out of all the problems on earth, the way the church expressed itself was through spiritual escapism. Escape the problems on earth, such as oppression, racism, injustice, police brutality, poverty, exploitation, inequality, so forth and so on. Most of the churches, black and white, put more emphasis on going to heaven than on doing God's will on earth. Saving the soul was the primary focus. Very rarely did you hear or see Christians concerned about the conditions that created the social, economic, and educational crisis in the community. When my eyes started to open, I could see the dichotomy of a preoccupation with heaven and a deemphasis on transforming the earth, which is a total contradiction of the gospel of Jesus Christ. Jesus taught and demonstrated "God's will on earth as it is in heaven." The purpose of Christianity was never a preoccupation with escaping the earth but transforming it. Walter Rauschenbusch stated, "The essential purpose of Christianity was to transform human society into the Kingdom of God by regenerating all human relations and reconstituting them in accordance with the will of God."[1] How can people expect to inherit heaven when they refuse to take responsibility on earth? How can they expect to enter into eternal rest when they refuse to enter into the conditions and situations of suffering people? How can they expect to hear the Savior say, "Well Done" when they have not done the work of the Kingdom of God? Until Christians and nonChristians take responsibility on earth, they won't inherit the heaven they desire to go to.

No matter how much people think of themselves as Christians, this does not equate to being saved and sanctified. Christian is a label and labels often don't convey the truth. For example, Eveready batteries are sold in many department stores to set them apart from other battery products. The label conveys the battery is ever ready. It is a sales pitch to get customers to buy this product over others. In reality, the battery does not do according to its sales pitch. No battery is ever ready all the time anytime. Therefore, the label is misleading. In like fashion, Christianity is a label meaning living and acting like Jesus Christ. But, in reality, those who claim to be Christian are a far cry from the label they wear. Look how racism, slavery, and oppression are still a reality in America that sees itself as predominantly Christian. Look how segregated churches are based on race. Many who wear the label Christian have no concern about justice: the poor, the oppressed, the weak, the vulnerable, and the marginalized. In the midst of social, economic, and educational injustice, it's Christians who cry the most for law and order while silent about structures of injustice. Many white catholic and evangelicals are silent about the George Floyds who are killed around the country by policemen. Being loud about law and order and silent about ordered injustice is causing the hemorrhaging influence of

---

1. Walter Rauschenbusch, *Christianity And The Social Crisis* (New York: The Macmillan Company, 1910), xiii.

not only American democracy but also American Christianity. Those who wear the label Christian and live the opposite of what it really means will be held accountable for their false advertisement.

There are two billion Christians in the world. Are all Christians looking forward to going to heaven? They are looking forward to a place where there is uninterrupted bliss and pleasure, and where—as the scripture points out, "The wolf will live with the lamb, the leopard will lie down with the goat, the calf and the lion and the yearling together; and a little child will lead them (Isaiah 11:6)." Other faiths such as Islam, Hinduism and Buddhism—are expecting to go to such a place as well. There is something innately within all people that yearns to go to a place better than where people are living now. We yearn for a place free of pain, suffering, violence, stress, and death. Nobody that I have come across wants to go to a place opposite to the description of heaven. Heaven is the utopian dream that people desire to go to after death or during the rapture. The most evil, unjust, vile, racist, and inhumane person on earth wants to go to heaven. If there were a slight possibility for Satan and all the demons of hell to enter into heaven, they would go. However, despite the great desire of people wanting to go to heaven, this reality will fall short for untold numbers of people. Their desire and destination won't match because everybody talking about heaven is not going there. Despite the doctrine of universalism—the belief that all souls will eventually go to heaven, the teachings of Jesus refute this very flawed, unbiblical conclusion. To conclude that all people, regardless of their beliefs and practices, will go to heaven is nothing short of intellectualism gone mad. This is the reason it is said there are fourteen inches between the head and heart, and many people will miss heaven by fourteen inches because people are trying to intellectualize a plausibility for universalism.

Notwithstanding, it is the will of God that all people are saved and enter into the Kingdom of God. For this reason, Christ delays his return because He does not desire "Any should perish but that all should come to repentance (2 Peter 3:9)." What God did through Christ was not "To condemn the world but that the world through him might be saved (John 3:17)." God desires for all people to be saved, but all people won't be saved because of their unbelief and consistent unrepentant rebellion. When people live in a state of disobedience and refuse to do the will of God, it is the influence of the doctrine of demons to believe that all people will go to heaven. Universalism is a lie that shouldn't be taught nor advanced by any preacher or teacher of the scriptures. If we are not born again by the Spirit of God, according to our Lord and Savior Jesus Christ, we won't see nor enter the Kingdom of God (John 3:3)." The number of people who desire to go to heaven with the small number who are actually born again, explains the reason untold many won't pass the test to make it in. As many religious practitioners there are, everybody is not born again and consequently won't see nor enter the Kingdom of God!

The talk of heaven can be heard across cultural and religious lines, but the problem is people are keeping the two mutually exclusive. They act the very opposite of where they desire to go. People are mean, evil, racist, sexist, hateful, unjust, ungodly, and callous, and live like hellions, yet they talk about going to a place opposite to how they live on earth. Shouldn't we act like where we desire to go? If I desire to go to Alaska, I won't pack my luggage with clothes like I am going to South Florida or the Bahamas. The inconsistency of the way people act and where they desire to go is staggering. There is an old cliche that says, "So heavenly bound but no earthly good." What an oxymoron. How can people think they are going to heaven when they are busy doing what Frank Sinatra's song called "My Way?" This is the great problem with modern mankind. People are busy doing it "My Way." As a result, mankind has been plunged into an unending holocaust of wars, countless loss of life, nagging oppression, frustrating racism, and overall man's inhumanity to man. "My Way" says the end justifies the means and might makes right. Sadly, many postmodern Christians have this same twisted psychology to believe that "My Way" is acceptable to God. They want a crown but no cross. They want religion but no responsibility. They want a savior but no sacrifice. It never ceases to amaze me that "People want the promises, not the Provider; they want the gifts, not the Giver; they want the blessings, not the Blesser."[2] They think going to church and participating in religious rites and ceremonies without a relationship with the Redeemer will still gain them entrance into

---

2. Reginald F Davis, *Transforming Faith to Shape the World Around Us* (Macon, GA: Nurturing Faith Inc., 2019), 18.

the Kingdom of God. They have never taken to heart what Jesus says, "I am the way, the truth, and the life (John 14:6). Doing it "My Way" is the reason American Christianity is messed up. It is the reason for the deep racial divide in the nation and the reason we have the Divided States of America instead of the United States of America.

It is amazing how people think they are going to heaven when they fail to "Do justly, love mercy, and walk humbly with God?" How can they go to heaven when they overlook the poor, ignore the cries of the oppressed, and remain silent in the face of glaring injustice? Since Christ involved himself in social justice, shouldn't Christians do likewise? Since Jesus gave himself for the liberation of the oppressed, should Christians do the same? Shouldn't Christians live like Good Samaritans on the road of life? Jesus would not have demonstrated these things had He not intended for His followers to do likewise. People's preoccupation with heaven has created what theologians call "quietism," a refusal to undertake corrective actions against social and economic injustice. This is what Karl Marx meant in speaking of religion as an "opiate," a drug that helps people to conform rather than transform structural injustice. Many Christian people sit back, say and do nothing in the face of racial injustice. They never think that their collective silence is complicity in the sin of racism and injustice and that this won't be weighted in the balance before Jesus Christ. They think acts of inhumanity towards people of color in the United States are just business as usual. Business as usual means no sense of urgency to correct wrong or injustice and requires no attention and serious discussion. Many Christians continue their way of life, not being moved at all by the injustice against the poor and oppressed because it is the normal cultural practice of the nation. Normality leads to insensitivity that leads to noninvolvement in transforming systemic racism. Racism hurts and destroys people. Yet, in all of this, many Christians see no need to repent from their personal and collective complicity in the ongoing sin of the nation. They rest on the assurance that they are saved because they believe, but belief is not enough if it doesn't produce obedience in doing the will of God. Jesus said, "Why do you call me, 'Lord, Lord,' and do not do what I say (Luke 6:46)?" Getting involved to help the vulnerable and the marginalized of society is the actions of those who say they believe. If we believe, we must act not only with our voices but with our hands, feet, and eyes to represent Christ in the affairs of humanity. However, "If the Church tries to confine itself to theology and the Bible, and refuses its larger mission to humanity, its theology will gradually become mythology and its Bible a closed book."[3] We must "Be doers of the word, and not hearers only (James 1:22)."

People often say, "When I get to heaven, I am going to sit down and rest all day." This is one of the reasons many people won't get to heaven. They have been sitting down resting while the nation and the world are going to hell in a handbasket. They have been comfortable praising the Lord with their lips, but their hearts and actions are far from the struggle against evil and injustice. They are waiting to go to heaven but refusing to take action on earth. They think heaven is a place of eternal leisure, a place where recipients are just sitting around idle, basking in the light of God's glory. The Bible doesn't support this theological viewpoint. The angels in heaven are not just sitting around being idle; they are serving the most High God. They are working to carry out the will of God. In his dream, Jacob saw "A ladder set up on the earth, the top of it reaching to heaven; and the angels of God were ascending and descending on it (Genesis 28:12)." The angels are working and executing their assignments. Therefore, what makes people think that heaven is about sitting around and being idle? People do enough of this on earth. This is why Jesus said, "The harvest is plentiful, but the workers are few (Matthew 9:37)." The workers are few because the majority of Christians are having church but not being the church. They are at ease with their church activities when the mission field of advancing the Kingdom of God is right in their backyard. Their immediate surrounding goes unattended because they have no real understanding of the good news of the Gospel of Jesus Christ. God spoke through the prophet Amos, saying, "Woe to them that are at ease in Zion. And those who feel secure on the mountain of Samaria (Amos 6:1)." Insomuch as God warns us about complacency, escapism, quietism, and spiritual laziness on earth, God will not tolerate it in heaven.

Moreover, if American Christianity is only an exercise in liturgical and ceremonial expressions, it's a dead religion. James said, "Religion that God our Father accepts as pure and faultless is this: to look after orphans and

---

3. Walter Rauschenbusch, *Christianity And The Social Crisis*, 339.

widows in their distress and to keep oneself from being polluted by the world (James 1:27)." Widows and orphans need justice; they need health care; they need advocacy to meet their needs in an unjust society. If religion and socioeconomic engagement remain exclusive of one another, all we have is a saltless pietism, which is not "Good for anything, except to be thrown out and trampled underfoot (Matthew 5:13)." Yet, we hear people talking about wearing crowns in heaven, but they escape bearing a cross on earth. We hear them talking about putting on shoes in heaven but refuse to help the shoeless people on earth. We hear them talking about putting on robes in heaven but do nothing to clothe the naked on earth. Martin Luther King, Jr. stated:

> It's all right to talk about "silver slippers over yonder," but men need shoes to wear down here. It's all right to talk about streets flowing with "milk and honey" over yonder, but let's get some food to eat for people down here in Asia and Africa and South America and in our own nation who go to bed hungry at night. It's all right to talk about "mansions in the sky," but I'm thinking about these ghettoes and slums right down here.[4]

True religion motivates people to do the will of God on earth as it is in heaven. So, whatever heaven is and wherever heaven is, it is not going anywhere. Heaven will be there for us if we make it in. What God needs are some willing hands, feet, eyes, and tongues right down here to be the leaven in the economic, social, and political lump of America for its transformation. We should be co-laboring with God, making justice and righteousness the pillars of our nation and the world. Scripture defines us as "Treasure in earthen vessels (2 Corinthians 4:7)." We are very valuable and necessary on earth. Chris Marshall stated, "Humans are created to be representatives of God—a kind of icon of God in the world. They are the means by which God's loving rule is to be made visible on earth. Since God is a God of justice, those who bear God's image must also be agents of justice. They are to learn from God what justice means and to reproduce what they learn in all their activities in the world."[5]

---

[4]. Cited From Lewis V. Baldwin, *To Make the Wounded Whole* (Minneapolis, MN: Fortress Press, 1992), 47.
[5]. Chris Marshall, The Little Book of *Biblical Justice* (Intercourse, PA, Good Books Publisher, 2005), 25–26.

However, to the chagrin of Christ, much of American Christianity is dough and not leaven. Instead of being what Apostle Paul described himself and the Philippians Christians as "A colony of heaven," the majority of evangelical Christians are supporters and guarantors of the status quo. Their non-action towards structural injustice shows their support of it. What you don't repudiate in action says you support in theory. This is not mere conjecture but factual. Jesus said, "You will know them by their fruits (Matthew 7:15)." American history reveals how American Christianity stood with and not against American slavery, and to this day, it is still complicit in the social and economic inequalities of the nation. American Christianity is not the Christianity of Christ. Many American Christians think they are practicing the Christianity of Christ when they are actually practicing American Christianity. American Christianity surrendered its prophetic mission early in the nation's history when it allowed the unquenchable thirst for power and wealth to twist its understanding of the church in society. When American Christianity went to bed with the oligarchs and plutocrats through the Enlightenment rationale of Thomas Hobbes and John Locke, it no longer had an identity with the Christianity of Christ. It became the right hand of unchecked capitalism and the defender of the rich against the poor. It oriented souls to otherworldly salvation while allowing the body of people to be used, abused, and accrued for the profits of the elite. It became a cultural religion indifferent to justice while advocating a "pie in the sky" compensation. Frederick Douglass saw through the thin veneer of American Christianity that disguised itself as the Christianity of Christ. Douglass made this acute observation:

> Between the Christianity of this land and the Christianity of Christ, I recognize the widest possible difference—so wide that to receive the one as good, pure, and holy is of necessity to reject the other as bad, corrupt, and wicked. To be a friend of the one is of necessity to be the enemy of the other . . . (American Christianity is) the corrupt, slaveholding, women-whipping, cradle-plundering, partial and hypocritical [religion] of this land.[6]

---

6. Frederick Douglass, *Narrative of the Life of Frederick Douglass, An American Slave* (Garden City: Anchor Books, 1973), Appendix, 153.

Had the American church practiced the Christianity of Christ, we would have a different America today. We wouldn't be bogged down in racial strife, division, and bitterness. We could have truly been a nation of American exceptionalism, but instead, we became a nation of American shame. The fact that American Christianity never became the Christianity of Christ, we are reaping the bitter fruit of racial hatred, denominational division, exploitation, violence, hostility, and death. Our nation is deeply split down race, class, and economic lines. The scripture says, "The fathers have eaten sour grapes and set the children's teeth on the edge (Ezekiel 18:2), which means that the (founding fathers, with the complicity of the Christian church) have messed up America. The seeds of racism, inequality, racial hatred, and violence were planted in American soil, and now we are reaping the harvest. Had the American church stood up against slavery, racism, greed, lawlessness, licentiousness, and lynching, the United States would not be shrouded in racial conflict and oppression. H. Richard Niebuhr said:

> The causes of the racial schism are not difficult to determine. Neither theology nor polity furnished the occasion for it. The sole source of this denominationalism is social; it demonstrates clearly the invasion of the church of Christ by the principle of caste. And this caste sense is, as always, primarily present in the economically and culturally superior group and secondarily, by reaction, in the economically and culturally inferior society.
>
> Negroes have apparently taken the initiative in forming separate churches, but the responsibility lies with their former masters in the North and South. These made the independent church movement inevitable by the attitude that they adopted toward the colored Christians. Their unquestioned assumption of superior privileges, their unconscious wounding of the Negro self-respect, their complacent acceptance of the morality of the world as fitting for the church, have once more divided the body of Christ along the lines of social class. . . . Caste hostility leads to inevitable suspicious and misunderstandings even in the church.[7]

---

7. H. Richard Niebuhr, *The Social Sources of Denominationalism* (New York: World Publishing, 1929), 260.

The way blacks were treated while worshipping among whites shows how we got to this point where we are today. American Christianity was at work, not the Christianity of Christ, which caused Richard Allen and others to leave the white church and start their own to avoid further indignities of whites. To this day, the church is still split down racial, class, and privileged lines. American Christianity apparently is not concerned that the split in the church is bringing about its eventual death in America. If there were a genuine concern, the ongoing injustices against blacks and people of color in America would be minimized, if not altogether eliminated. If the institutions of our land topple and fall, so will the church that held them up. Had American Christianity practiced religion in the biblical sense of the word, we would be a model of true democracy and equality of diversity. Jemar Tisby stated, "Things could have been different. At several points in American history—the colonial era, Reconstruction, the demise of Jim Crow—Christians could have confronted racism instead of compromising."[8] Due to the fact that American Christianity stood for and still stands with unjust social structures, the gospel message of Jesus Christ is made to be of no effect.

In his book *America's Unholy Ghost,* Joel Edward Goza states three lies that led to America's religious and theological racism. His analysis shows that American Christianity was duped into believing that it could have a vertical relationship with God without a horizontal relationship with humankind.

> The first religious lie that shaped America's white church was that Christians could be in the right relationship with their God without being in the right relationship with the broken and abused of their society. The lie contradicted both the Old and New Testaments. . . . The second lie tightly aligned to the first: religion is about the salvation of the soul. This lie was Locke's as he labored to institutionalize enlightened ideas regarding religion in ways that protected and perpetuated society's social divides. "The only business of the Church," as Locke said, "is the salvation of souls; and it no way concerns the commonwealth, or any member of it. . . . The third lie: indifference to injustice is no threat to one's intimacy

---

8. Jemar Tisby, *The Color of Compromise* (Grand Rapids, MI: Zondervan, 2019), 18.

with God. In biblical traditions, indifference to injustice means one really doesn't know the Bible's God, and it leads Jesus to damn the indifferent to "the eternal fire prepared for the devil and his angels."[9]

There is no question that American Christianity became the justifier of the unjust social, economic and political practice of this land. It is still the silent on-looker of structural injustice while millions of people of color are constant victims of racism, police brutality, and deferred dreams. Howard Thurman stated, "It cannot be denied that too often the weight of the Christian movement has been on the side of the strong and the powerful and against the weak and oppressed—this, despite the gospel."[10] This was James Cone's theological resentment of white theologians who never made the suffering of the oppressed their point of departure in doing theology. The suffering of African Americans during and after slavery was ignored and made invisible, leaving them with no theological protection against religious bigotry and violence.

The cultural norms of society—even though these norms are antithetical to the Kingdom of God—are still not challenged by American Christianity. The tilt of American Christianity still leans towards the rich and powerful. It still gives legitimation to the arrangement of society. Most American Christians don't question nor understand the tilt of their religious practice. They go along with the tradition that links the American culture of patriotism party politics, with their national religion of American Christianity. As long as everything is whitewashed, and there isn't anything to threaten the arrangement of white supremacy and its acts of violence, American Christianity is just as guilty of racism and oppression. Because it supports the socioeconomic structure of society, it is part of the problem an ongoing enemy to the Kingdom of God. America's religion can be described in the words of Peter Berger:

> Religion legitimates social institutions by bestowing upon them an ultimately valid ontological status, that is, by locating them within a sacred and cosmic frame of reference. . . . Let the institutional order be

---

9. Joel Edward Goza, *America's Unholy Ghost The Racist Roots of Our Faith and Politics* (Eugene, OR: Cascade Books an Imprint of Wipf and Stock Publishers, 2019), 147.
10. Howard Thurman, *Jesus and the Disinherited* (Friends United Press, 1981), 31.

> so interpreted as to hide, as much as possible, its constructed [human character]. . . . Let the people forget that this order was established by men and continues to be dependent upon the consent of men. Let them believe that, in acting out the institutional programs that have been imposed upon them, they are but realizing the deepest aspirations of their own being and putting themselves in harmony with the fundamental order of the universe.[11]

The reason it is very difficult to achieve justice and equality, American Christianity believes that God is on their side. But, the question is which god. Oppression, racism, and exploitation are surely not the aid and abetting of the God of Jesus Christ. The God of Jesus Christ works against these things in human society. Therefore, we have to conclude that American slavery, which lasted for three and a half centuries, was not the action and power of God but man. Americans may appeal to a god, but it surely isn't the Most High God. The American church allowed itself to be manipulated by the power elite, who twisted the scriptures to fit their benefits. Although physical slavery is no longer lawful in America, its residual effects are still with the nation today. American Christianity today is still, by and large, about protecting the interest of the powerful against the powerless while talking about a Jesus they have created who is not in any way, form or fashion engaged in the socioeconomic structure of society for its transformation. However, the abolitionist movement and the civil rights movement attempted to inject the Christianity of Christ into the veins of American Christianity, but the body politic rejected the transfusion.

Yet, in America, if a poll was taken today, a great majority of American Christians not only believe in heaven but are sure they are going there. Despite the wrong, evil, and injustice that are glaringly in front of them, despite racism, poverty, homelessness, and inequality that surround them, and despite police brutality in the name of "law and order," many American Christians still believe their non-involvement won't affect them from entering into the Kingdom of God. They will quickly confess their belief in the existence of God. They believe all it takes is saying the sinners' prayers, believing in God and Jesus Christ as Savior, and they are sure to go to heaven. What they don't understand is if there is no heart transformation

---

11. Peter Berger, *The Sacred Canopy* (New York: Doubleday, 1969) 33.

and spiritual rebirth, they are just participating in a ceremonial rite that leads them back to business as usual. It is true that we are not saved by works, but by grace through faith, lest anyone should boast (Ephesians 2:8). However, James says, "You believe that there is one God. You do well. Even the demons believe—and tremble! (James 2:19)." To believe in God is not enough if it doesn't motivate us "To loose the chains of injustice and untie the cords of the yoke, to set the oppressed free and break every yoke (Isaiah, 58:6)." It is not enough if it doesn't motivate us to practice the "Pure and undefiled religion before God and the Father . . . to visit orphans and widows in their trouble, and to keep oneself unspotted from the world (James 1:27)." If we truly believe in God then we must act on this belief by being obedient to God through Jesus Christ. Many Christians don't won't to talk about racial injustice and oppression. Some may say, "Get over it—that's in the past." But, the past impacts the present, especially if the past issue has not been corrected. We can only get over past issues when we actually confront and correct them. How can a nation get over its sickness if it refuses to confront it? How can America provide a vaccine for racism when she doesn't acknowledge that this is a serious virus? Only when a nation acknowledges and confronts its sickness will she seek a doctor, and Dr. Jesus is the Balm in Gilead who can "Heal a sin-sick soul and make the wounded whole."

Jesus puts us on notice that everybody talking about heaven is not going there. "Not everyone who says to Me, 'Lord, Lord,' shall enter the kingdom of heaven, but he who does the will of My Father in heaven. Many will say to Me in that day, 'Lord, Lord, have we not prophesied in Your name, cast out demons in Your name, and done many wonders in Your name?' And then I will declare to them, 'I never knew you; depart from Me, you who practice lawlessness!'(Matthew 7:21-23)." Despite people's confessions and preoccupation with heaven, many of them are not going there. After attending church on Sunday, taking care of ecclesiastical functions, giving their money, and doing all of the religious duties, many will hear the disappointing voice of the Savior saying, "Depart from me, you who practiced lawlessness." Those who had a form of godliness but denied the power of God to transform their lives won't be allowed in. Those who used religion to justify racism, oppression, exploitation, greed, and white supremacy cannot enter. Those who never severed their relationship with a system that was predicated upon favoring the rich over the poor, the powerful over the powerless, and the strong over the weak, access will be denied into the Kingdom of heaven.

Countless people will be terrified when they find out they are actually going to hell instead of heaven. American Christianity is the vehicle that drove them away from the Kingdom of God. Like the Pharisees in Jesus's time, many Christians have made position, power, and privilege more important than the Kingdom of God. On the great day of accountability, Christ will disown many. When the secrets of all hearts shall be manifest, the result is many who say, "Lord, Lord, shall not enter into the Kingdom of God." They won't make it because they were self-deceived in being saved in their heads and not in their hearts. Paul wrote of this to the Romans. "For I bear them witness that they have a zeal for God, but not according to knowledge. For they being ignorant of God's righteousness, and seeking to establish their own righteousness, have not submitted to the righteousness of God (Romans 10:2-3)." How often does American Christianity submit to its own righteousness and not the righteousness of God? How often does the Christian church show it has never been born gain? Jesus told Nicodemus, "Most assuredly, I say to you, unless one is born again, he cannot see the kingdom of God (John 3:3)." America must be born again to see and enter into the Kingdom of God.

Looking at the present state of America and seeing its current practice of racism, sexism, classism, militarism, quietism, etc., there is no wonder many will be lost. This is the reason Martin Luther King, Jr. stated:

> One day, we will have to stand before the God of history, and we will talk in terms of things we've done. Yes, we will be able to say we built gargantuan bridges to span the seas; we built gigantic buildings to kiss the skies. Yes, we made our submarines to penetrate oceanic depths. We brought into being many other things with our scientific and technological power. It seems that I can hear the God of history saying, "That was not enough! But I was hungry and ye fed me not. I was naked, and ye clothed me not. I was devoid of a decent sanitary house to live in, and ye provided no shelter for me. And, consequently, you cannot enter the Kingdom of greatness. If ye do it unto the least of these, my brethren, ye do it unto me."[12]

---

12. Martin Luther King, Jr., *A Testament Of Hope The Essential Writings of Martin Luther King, Jr.*, edited by James Melvin Washington (San Francisco: Harper & Row Publishers, 1986), 275.

Unless the vertical relationship with God connects with the horizontal relationship with humankind, religion is vain. It is not real. "If someone says, "I love God," and hates his brother, he is a liar; for he who does not love his brother whom he has seen, how can he love God whom he has not seen? And this commandment we have from Him: that he who loves God *must* love his brother also (1 John 4:20-21)." Without love and concern for others, we won't inherit the Kingdom of God. Jesus says, "To whom much is given, much will be required (Luke 12:48)." The doing and giving of justice is a universal divine requirement. Without giving justice to others when it's in our power to do so, we won't inherit the Kingdom of God. James says, "Suppose a brother or a sister is without clothes and daily food. If one of you says to them, "Go in peace; keep warm and well fed," but does nothing about their physical needs, what good is it? (James 2:15-16)." Until America reorders her values and "Seek first the Kingdom of God and His righteousness (Matthews 6:33)," she won't enter the Lord's Kingdom. On earth certain names and money can gain people access to very powerful people and places. It can gain people access to one of the most powerful houses in the world, the White House. Not so with the Kingdom of God. People cannot buy their way into the Kingdom of God. They cannot bribe nor politic their way in. They cannot work, sing, and shout their way in. Unless people are rooted and grounded in Jesus Christ and do the will of God, the door of God's Kingdom will be shut to them.

Jesus says only those who do the will of God will gain access to the Kingdom of God. This begs the question. What is the Will of the Father? The Will of the Father is to believe in the Son of God and obey the gospel He brought to us. What is it that America has not yet obeyed? She has not set the captives free, healed the brokenhearted, or given justice to the poor, the oppressed, widows and orphans. She has not turned away from her racism and transformed her unjust social and economic structures. It is not the Will of the Father to just give charity. The Will of the Father is justice, and "Let it roll down like waters and righteousness like a mighty stream (Amos 5:24)." The Will of the Father is to transform the unjust system of society to be in line with the Kingdom of God. White America must do more than just be charitable. Warren W. Wiersbe stated:

We are handicapped in the white church. If I preached Jesus' first sermon (Luke 4:14-30 and gave it the social emphasis that He gave, our church would have no vehicle for doing anything about the problem. People would respond in one of two ways: 1) "This preacher is off-base, so let's get rid of him," or 2) "I've never seen it quite that way, but what do I do next?" For the most part, our white churches don't have the instruments, the organizational structure, to get involved in social action. Our usual solution is to put some inner-city organization into the budget or maybe to collect and distribute used clothing . . . When it comes to racial issues, many white churches will participate in any number of symbolic activities, but they're hesitant when you ask them to get involved in sacrificial services in the trenches.[13]

The Black Church, too, must look at the aim of its religious activities. If these activities are more about having church than about being the church, then it also will be held accountable at the judgment seat of Jesus Christ. James H. Cone made this observation about the black church:

Unfortunately, many contemporary black churches have strayed from their liberating heritage. Instead of deepening their commitment to the poor in their community and the Third World, many have adopted the same attitude toward the poor as have the white churches from which they separated. Too many black churches are more concerned about buying and building new church structures than they are about feeding, clothing, and housing the poor. If black churches do not repent by reclaiming their liberating heritage for the empowerment of the poor today, their Christian identity will be no more authentic than that of the white churches that segregated them.[14]

Unfortunately, many people will be surprised at the pronouncement of condemnation. Many will be shocked that they are denied entrance into the Kingdom of God. Others will be deeply disappointed that out of all the

---

13. E. K. Bailey and Warren W. Wiersbe, *Preaching in Black and White: What We Can Learn from Each Other* (Grand Rapids, MI: Zondervan, 2003), 105.

14. James H. Cone, *Speaking The Truth, Ecumenism, Liberation, and Black Theology* (Maryknoll, NY: Orbis Books, 1986), 122.

work they have done, they won't make it to heaven. They thought because of their work, they deserved to go to heaven. Many might say, "I was the president of this; I was the chairman of that," as if this is going to get them into the Kingdom of God. Do you hear these surprised people boasting that day? Their whole claim to Heaven rests on what they have done. In his work *The Unsaved Christian,* Dean Inserra stated that the reliance of many people on Jesus can translate to our era like this:

> Didn't we "say grace" before dinner? Didn't we vote our values?
> Didn't we believe prayer should be allowed in school?
> Didn't we go to church? Didn't we believe in God?
> Didn't we get misty eyes whenever we heard "God Bless America" sung at a baseball game? Didn't we give money to the church?
> Didn't we treat women with respect? Didn't we own Bibles?
> Didn't we get the baby christened by the priest? Didn't we want America to return to its Christian roots? Didn't we stay married and faithful?"[15]

These self-righteous people were so caught up in themselves they never repented from the thin veer of religiosity rooted in American Christianity. They could not pass the faith audit of the Righteous Judge. When they are weighed in the balance and found wanting, they will find out that their accomplishments were about them and not about Jesus Christ. Their race, class, and privileges trumped their love for Jesus Christ. They will find out that the "Lust of the flesh, and the lust of the eyes, and the pride of life (1 John 2:16) disqualified them from entering the Kingdom of God.

Moreover, this is one time the following statement is true and relevant, "It's not what you know but who you know." Harry Emerson Fosdick stated, "Ah, we respectable Christians! We have gone on building churches, elaborating complicated creeds, worshipping through splendid rituals, but how often the real spirit of Jesus has been somewhere else!"[16] One thing is clear: once the dreaded words of the Savior are pronounced to many, "Depart from Me," there won't be any appellate nor supreme court in

---

15. Dean Inserra, *The Unsaved Christian Reaching Cultural Christianity with the Gospel* (Chicago: Moody Publishers, 2019), 16–17.
16. Harry Emerson Fosdick, *Answers To Real Problems: Harry Emerson Fosdick Speaks To Our Time,* edited by Mark E. Yurs (Eugene, OR: Wipf & Stock Publishers, 2008), 39.

heaven nor on earth to reverse the verdict. "If these [words] do not strike terror in your heart, at least they should motivate serious apprehension about your destiny. Unfortunately, our minds seem to come up with the most amazing mental gymnastics to avoid dealing with these clear statements. We attempt to paint God in such a way that He could never be so harsh. This was the same error made by Adam and Eve in the Garden. It would be interesting to find out what the people who lived at the time of Noah would have said if they had heard the message that a flood that would destroy the whole world was coming. They might have imagined that God would not do such a thing, yet the flood came exactly when and how it was predicted."[17] There were probably many during the time of Noah who thought that God would not be that harsh to drown people, but we know that is exactly what happened. Repent before it is too late! "Depart from Me!" will be spoken, and it will be done.

---

17. William Wilberforce, *Real Christianity, Revised and Updated by Bob Beltz* (Ventura, CA: Regal Publisher, 1797), 109.

Chapter Two

HEAVEN IS FOR PREPARED PEOPLE

> *For all your days, be prepared and meet them ever alike. When you are the anvil, bear—when you are the hammer, strike.*
>
> —Edwin Markham

Scientists believe that global warning is causing extreme weather changes in our world, and with the number of hurricanes and thunderstorms we have had over the past few years, we cannot dispute the science. However, is it simply a global warning or the fulfillment of prophecy? Many believe it is both. There is no doubt we are living in the end times, as Jesus pointed out in Matthew 25th chapter. He also warned us to be ready for His coming in Matthew 24th chapter. The frequency of bad weather is costing America and the nations of the world hundreds of billions of dollars. Technology is providing information to help people prepare for upcoming hurricanes like never before. When hurricanes are looming near, there are often long lines in grocery and hardware stores where people are buying certain items they need to help them through the storm. People really get in a hurry responding to the flashing news about coming hurricanes and thunderstorms, but very few people—if any—respond in a hurry to the gospel news about the nearness of the return of Jesus Christ. You would think churches would be filled to capacity with people to hear how to prepare for the return of

Jesus Christ as they fill grocery and hardware stores to prepare for a coming storm. Very few people, including the ones that are members in the church, take serious the news of the return of Jesus Christ and how to prepare for His coming!

Now, there isn't anything wrong with preparing for a storm, but people also need to prepare for God's Kingdom to come in its fullness. Preparation to preserve physical life is necessary, and preparation for the salvation of the soul is also necessary. Preparation for the eternal destination of the soul should take precedence over everything else. But, too many people are busy taking care of the needs of the body while forgetting the needs of their souls. People are so caught up preparing for the physical life that they have no time for the spiritual life. And, what does it profit a man, a woman, a people, and a nation to gain the whole world and lose their souls (Mark 8:36)? People need to prepare for the Kingdom to come. The signs of the times are here to remind us at any time, in any place, Jesus Christ may appear. The scriptures point out that certain things will be happening as a precursor to the return of Jesus Christ. There will be earthquakes in different places. There will be wars and rumors of wars. There will be false prophets, famines, pestilences, and social chaos. A major sign is the restoration of the nation of Israel, the mark of the beast technology, the forming of the new world order, so forth and so on. All of these signs are unfolding before our very eyes, yet people are not rushing to prepare for God's Kingdom to come like they are rushing to the grocery and hardware stores to prepare for a hurricane.

If Christ would suddenly come today, and one day He suddenly will, I am afraid most people will be unprepared to meet Him. In the same vein, C. H. Spurgeon believed the carelessness of many people will render them unprepared when the Lord comes:

> Alas! How many put off all thoughts of being prepared . . . ! They are prepared for almost ready. You never will be ready, I fear. The carelessness in which you have lived so long has become habitual. One would think you had resolved to die in your sins. Have you ever heard the story of Archaeus, the Grecian despot, who was going to a feast, and on the way, a messenger brought him a letter and seriously importuned him to read

it? It contained tidings of a conspiracy that had been formed against him, that he would be killed at the feast. He took the letter and put it in his pocket. In vain, the messenger urged that it was concerning serious matters. "Serious matters tomorrow," said Archaeus, "feasting tonight." That night the dagger reached his heart while he had about him the warning which, had he heeded it, would have averted the peril. Alas! too many men say, "Serious things tomorrow!" They have no misgiving that when their sport is over, they will have alike the leisure and the leanings for these weighty matters. Were it not wiser, Sirs, to let these grave affairs come first? Might you not, then, find some better sport of nobler character than all the froth and frivolity to which fashion leads on? a holy merriment and a sacred feasting that well become immortal spirits. . . . Reck you not that time is short, that life is precarious, that opportunities cross your path at lightning speed, that hope flatters those on whom the fangs of death are fixed, that there is no vestibule in which to fit your frame of mind, that the shock will always come sudden at last. What sentence more trite, what sentiment more prevalent, yet what solemnity more neglected than this, "Prepare to meet your God"! Propound it, profess it, preach it as we may; the most of men are unprepared.[1]

Since America claims to be a Christian nation, many people are unprepared to meet the Lord. When we look around our nation and the world, there are human conditions so inhumane and unjust that the abysmal failure of the church and government is very apparent. When the church and government have failed the people, they are a failure before Jesus Christ. Instead of the church being the moral conscience and righteous gadfly to the nation, the church is caught up in the cares of this world that distracts it from paying attention to the signs of the times. It seems the church has traded the Kingdom of God's mandates for the fleeting pleasures of this world. Over the years, the church has compromised with the world and lost its prophetic voice, leaving unjust social and economic structures untouched.

There are churches on almost every corner of American society, yet many of these corners are overrun with poverty, crime, violence, drugs,

---

1. C.H. Spurgeon, "Preparation For Heaven" No. 3538 Sermon at Metropolitan Tabernacle Pulpit, Newington, Published on November 16, 1916, Vol. 62.

prostitution, unemployment, indifference, hopelessness, etc. Very rarely is there transformation because too many Christians refuse to really get involved in the life of these places. They refuse to challenge the states that allow such conditions to exist in these places. Many Christians would rather talk about a heaven they have never been to than help transform the lives of people right down here on earth. Religion, when it is authentic, is to care for the poor, widows, orphans, and the least of these. It not only deals with the symptoms but the causes of poverty and injustice. When religion is only concerned about souls and not the communities in which people live their lives, religion is no more than a sedative to help people escape their reality. American Christianity has become a private instead of social engagement. There is much talk about the separation of church and state. God never meant for His people to separate the moral law from the state. We are to bring to bear God's laws to the state and nation so we can create a just and moral nation. Therefore, our Judeo-Christian religion should be more public than private. The prophets publicly preached the oracles of God. Jesus publicly demonstrated the Kingdom of God. Publicly, we are to bring to bear the Kingdom of God upon the socioeconomic and political life of the nation. John Wesley said, "Christianity is essentially a social religion, and to turn it into a solitary religion is indeed to destroy it."[2] Private religion is a total contradiction of the life and ministry of Jesus Christ. Jesus was always prepared and ready to repair the torn fabric of society, and no church can do this in the community if it is not involved in the community. The church as a whole still does not in any significant way deal with all the social, economic, educational, medical, and political ills of the community and nation, and life is getting worse for many people in America and the world.

Now, when Jesus Christ returns and finds the world in the condition it is in today, what would be the excuses of the people of faith? How would we explain to the Lord the present conditions of the nation and our failure to transform at least our community? Would we confess that life might have been better for people had we acted with intentionality? Would we confess that because of the deceitfulness of wealth, we allowed justice to lay prostrate on the ground? Would we confess racial division in the church

---

2. John Wesley, *The Quotable Wesley by Dave Armstrong* (Kansas City: Beacon Hill Press, 2014), 52.

was a result of refusing to see ourselves as one in the Body of Christ? What excuse would we render for the silence of not taking a stand for racial and social injustice?

Furthermore, would our excuses and confessions be enough to gain us access to the Kingdom of God? According to the scriptures, the answer is a resounding no! Our Lord warned us in scripture the punishment for being unprepared. Jesus made it clear that when He returns, and we are not prepared, we must suffer the consequences. On more than one occasion, Jesus told His hearers about the consequences of being unprepared. Jesus warned the hearers that one day, He could come when people least expected him. "Watch, therefore, for you do not know what hour your Lord is coming. But know this, that if the master of the house had known what hour the thief would come, he would have watched and not allowed his house to be broken into. Therefore, you also be ready, for the Son of Man is coming at an hour you do not expect (Matthew 24:42-44)." In Mark 13:35-37 Jesus said, "Watch therefore, for you do not know when the master of the house is coming—in the evening, at midnight, at the crowing of the rooster, or in the morning—lest, coming suddenly, he find you sleeping. And what I say to you, I say to all: Watch!" These and other scriptures point out there is no excuse accepted for not being prepared and sleeping at the Lord's coming. The cost is an eternal regret.

To further take the seriousness of His coming, Jesus used a parable to help us understand His unannounced coming. Jesus tells the parable of ten virgins found in the 25th chapter of Matthew. The ten virgins all heard and understood the bridegroom was coming one day. They all believed He was coming. The time of His coming is unknown, but they were assured that one day, He will come as He said. The thing to do is to prepare for His coming. Although the ten virgins heard the same news, they had the same expectations and the same opportunity. Five of them prepared and the other five delayed. Just like today! People have been hearing about the return of Jesus Christ; they know one day, He is coming.

The church has been singing for years, "Soon and very soon, we are going to see the King," but like the ten virgins, people respond differently to what they have heard. People fall into two categories. They are either wise or foolish—yet consider themselves Christians. They will either enter into life with the bridegroom or be locked out of life because they were unprepared to meet the bridegroom. When the five wise virgins heard the news of the coming bridegroom, they immediately started to prepare. They didn't take for granted what they heard. They didn't take the position that they were too busy, and that it is not that urgent, and they have time. They used time wisely. They understood that anticipation and preparation can be strangled by procrastination that ends up as spiritual stagnation ultimately causing damnation. The five wise virgins didn't just talk about getting ready; they were actively preparing themselves every day. They were not sitting around talking about what they needed to do; they did it. They didn't just talk about love; they demonstrated love; they didn't just meet about justice; they practiced it. They didn't talk about feeding the hungry, clothing the naked, or providing shelter for the homeless; they did it. They didn't talk about evangelism; they carried it out. They didn't talk about standing up against wrong, evil, and injustice; they stood up against these things. They didn't meet about how much oil it would take; they made sure they had enough in their lamps. They prioritized the coming bridegroom and never allowed their expectation to wear down over time. Every day, they were putting their faith in action, believing the bridegroom might come at anytime.

In the preparation process, they didn't get caught up in worldly distractions; they didn't maximize the minimum and minimize the maximum. They had their priorities right and never allowed themselves to get sucked in by the suction tube of an ungodly culture. They took time to cut off the loose edges of the rags in the lamp and saturated them with fresh oil to be prepared in case the bridegroom called. Not only did they trim the loose edges of the rags in the lamp, but they also adjusted the wick within. To make sure the light wouldn't go out, they carried extra oil. They constantly adjusted their lamps and did what they needed to do to stay prepared for the coming of the bridegroom. These wise virgins stayed ready. Throughout the vicissitudes of life, they constantly prepared. They prepared for tomorrow's eternity by getting ready for it today. The five wise virgins stayed alert. They prepared physically and spiritually. They were born again; they were faithful; they were obedient and doing the Will of God while waiting for the expected call of the bridegroom. They waited in anticipation! Like spare tires kept in cars, the wise virgins kept extra oil in their lamps just in case when the bridegroom called at night; they would have enough oil to make the journey to keep the lamps burning. Then, one day, the long-expected event happened! "At midnight, a cry was heard: 'Behold, the bridegroom is coming; go out to meet him (Matthew 25:6)!" The wise virgins were ready and prepared to meet Him, and they went into the wedding feast with the bridegroom and the door was shut.

Now, the five foolish virgins were caught unprepared. Instead of using time wisely, time became their enemy. Time ran out for them, and they were shut out of the marriage feast. They believed in the coming of the bridegroom, but time ran out; they meant to prepare, but time ran out. They were talking about the wedding feast, but time ran out. They had a lot of meetings about what they needed to do but never got it done; they talked about love but didn't demonstrate it; they talked about forgiveness but never extended it; they talked about reconciliation but never made an effort. They talked about justice and equality, but it ended up being mere lip service. They made the Christian confession but failed in Christian commitment. The five foolish virgins postponed preparation, believing they had time; time to love; time to correct oppression; time to end racism; time to reform an unjust criminal justice system; time to feed the hungry, clothe the naked; and provide shelter for the homeless. They knew their oil lamps of love, compassion, justice, and obedience were low, but believing they had time, they put off purchasing more. They didn't prioritize the coming bridegroom. At midnight, when the cry was heard, "The bridegroom is coming. Go out and meet him." The foolish virgins were not prepared. In their desperation to meet the bridegroom, they said to the wise virgins, "Give us some of your oil; our lamps are going out." But, the wise said, "No, there may not be enough for both us and you. Instead, go to those who sell oil and buy some for yourselves." The bridegroom came and the wise virgins were ready and went in with Him to the wedding, and the door was shut. When the foolish virgins came back from purchasing more oil, the door was shut, and they knocked and knocked and knocked, saying, "Lord, Lord, open the door for us." But He answered, "I don't know you!"

Notwithstanding, this will be the saying to many unprepared people knocking at the door of eternal life, and the reply shall be, "I don't know you!" Many religious Americans will plead, "Lord, we were good Christians; we believed in democracy; we believed in a more perfect union; we saluted the American flag and gave money to charities. We confess that we could have done a better job about structural racism, inequality, white supremacy, voter suppression, and the exploitation of the poor. We confess that black life, black suffering, black theology, and the poor were made invisible in our churches, seminaries, and churches. We knew our forefathers were wrong in what they did to the poor, the oppressed, and the black race. We also knew the Kerner Report of 1968 the government conducted was our responsibility to correct. We knew and understood:

> Our nation is moving toward two societies, one black, one white—separate and unequal. Racial prejudice, discrimination and segregation have shaped our history decisively; they now threaten the future of every American. Why did it happen? Certain fundamental matters are clear. Of these, the most fundamental is the racial attitude and behavior of white Americans toward black Americans . . . White racism is essentially responsible . . . What white Americans have never fully understood, but what the Negro can never forget—is that white society is deeply implicated in the ghetto. White institutions created it, white institutions maintain it, and white society condones it.[3]

We knew that racism is deeply implicated in the ghetto, and we should have moved from confession to correction. We should have solved these problems, but we made excuses. We also confess that our Christianity was infected with what William R. Jones called 'Whiteanity' that guarantees oppression's successful disguise, not its demise.[4] We confess that we did not commit ourselves to wipe out every visage of wrong, evil, and injustice against the oppressed, not even in our religious tradition. Lord, forgive us! We believed in the oneness of humanity; we were just slow in demonstrating it in our nation. We could have consistently worked to reform our criminal justice system; we could have reformed the police departments

---

3. Report of the National Advisory Commission on Civil Discover, U.S. Government Printing Office, 1968, 1.
4. William R. Jones, *Is God A White Racists, A Preamble to Black Theology* (Boston, MA: Beacon Press Books, 1998), x.

that shot and killed unarmed black people. We could have passed gun legislation to prevent the further loss of lives. We confess our complicity in an unjust system, and we intend to correct it. Sometimes, we talked about it, but then other interests came along, and we pushed it back into invisibility. We were in the process of making these issues our top priority, but Lord, you appeared before we could do it." Others will probably plea, "We went to church; we attended Sunday School and Bible study. We made sure our children were in vacation Bible school. Lord Have Mercy! We meant to pray; we meant to repent; we meant to fight racism and correct oppression; we meant 'To do justly, love mercy, and walk humbly with God (Micah 6:8).'" But, no amount of pleas will be accepted by the Lord. William D. Watley stated that these "meant to" excuses won't be acceptable.

> There are a lot of people who will end up in hell because of "meant to" religion. We meant to visit the sick; we meant to ask our neighbors' forgiveness. We meant to say a kind word. We meant to go to church; we certainly meant to keep all those promises we made when we were sick. We meant to be a good Christian husband or wife, son or daughter, father or mother—be we just became sidetracked. We became so engrossed in doing what we wanted to do that we kept putting it off . . . Meant to religion has never done anything but talk. It has never saved a soul, comforted the sick, or repaired any hurt feelings.[5]

Jesus shall say, "I don't know you! I told you to 'Watch therefore, for you know neither the day nor the hour in which the Son of Man is coming.'" Many people, especially Christians, will be surprised to hear the Master say, "I don't know you." They will not enter because they were not prepared. They were shut out because the Kingdom of God is for prepared people; not religious people but prepared people; not old and young people but prepared people; not working and retired people but prepared people; not church people but prepared people; not educated people but prepared people; not uneducated people but prepared people; not rich people but prepared people; not poor people but prepared people; not conservative or liberal, republican or democratic people but prepared people; not black or

---

5. William D. Watley, *Sermons on Special Days* (Valley Forge, PA: Judson Press, 1987), 99–100.

white people but prepared people. If people are not prepared, it is too late when the Lord comes. This parable "Warns us that there are certain things which cannot be obtained at the last minute. It is far too late for a student to be prepared when the day of the examination has come. It is too late for a man to acquire a skill or a character if he does not already possess it when some task offers itself to him."[6] It is too late to repair the roof when the rain is falling. It is too late to jump back once the jump is made off a skyscraper. It is too late to withdraw a hand once it is caught in a wood grinder. It is too late to trim the wick and get more oil when the call is heard. The point is once the call comes to meet the bridegroom, it is too late to prepare, too late to repent, too late to straighten up and fly right.

The foolish virgins were not prepared to meet the Lord and, therefore, could not enter into the Kingdom of Greatness. They asked the wise virgins to give them some oil, but there are some things in life people must do for themselves. There are some things we cannot give. We cannot give people character, growth, and maturity. We cannot give people a relationship with God. We cannot give people transformed hearts; they must do these things for themselves. This parable "Warns us that there are certain things which cannot be borrowed. The foolish virgins found it impossible to borrow oil when they discovered they needed it. A man cannot borrow a relationship with God; he must possess it for himself. A man cannot borrow a character; he must be clothed with it. We cannot always be living on the spiritual capital which others have amassed. There are certain things we must win or acquire for ourselves, for we cannot borrow them from others."[7]

Therefore, we must prepare to meet the Lord because He may come when we least expect him. A cosmic call has gone out across the world that the Lord is coming. Are we prepared to meet the Lord? Do we have enough oil in our lamps? Once the door of eternal life has shut, no excuse is acceptable to open it. Just like the door of Noah's Ark could not be opened when the flood waters came, the door to the Kingdom of God will not be opened regardless of the knocks and pleas. Be on the alert! Don't put off preparation for eternal habitation by procrastination. Martin Luther King, Jr. stated, "In this unfolding conundrum of life and history, there is such a thing as

---

6. William Barclay, "Commentary on Matthew 25:4," *William Barclay's Daily Study Bible*, viewed at https://www.studylight.org/commentaries/dsb/matthew-25.htm138, 1956–1959.

7. Ibid, Barclay Commentary on Matthew 25.

being too late. Procrastination is still the thief of time. Life often leaves us standing bare, naked and dejected with a lost opportunity. The 'tide in the affairs of men' does not remain at the flood; it ebbs. We may cry out desperately for time to pause in her passage, but time is deaf to every plea and rushes on. Over the bleached bones and jumbled residues of numerous civilizations are written the pathetic words: 'Too late.' There is an invisible book of life that faithfully records our vigilance or our neglect."[8] It is a poor tradeoff to give attention to temporal things for eternal things. Alfred Lord Tennyson, the great British poet, put this parable in graphic terms to remind us about waiting too late to know the cost of being unprepared:

> Late, late so late! and dark the night and chill!
> Late, late so late! but we can enter still.
> Too late, too late! ye cannot enter now.
> No light had we; for that we do repent;
> And learning this, the bridegroom will relent.
> No light: so late! and dark and chill the night!
> O let us in, that we may find the light!
> Too late, too late: ye cannot enter now.
> Have we not heard the bridegroom is so sweet?
> O let us in, tho' late, to kiss his feet!
> No, no, too late! ye cannot enter now."[9]

There is an eternal price to pay when we take for granted the urgency to be prepared when the Lord calls. A.W. Tozer made a profound statement about expectation and preparation:

> ... the Lord may soon return. I realize there is a lot that we do not know about prophecy, but most Christians are looking for the second coming of the Lord. They expect him to come. They do not know when He will come, and the ones who claim they do, do not. Nevertheless, He may come in your life time. He said He would come back in an hour, we

---

8. Martin Luther King, Jr., *Where Do We Go From Here: Chaos or Community, A Testament of Hope, The Essential Writings of Martin Luther, King, Jr.*, edited by James Melvin Washington (San Francisco: Harper & Row Publishers, 1986), 633.

9. Ibid, Barclay Commentary on Matthew 25.

think not. It could be that this present decline in expectation may have an ominous significance. It can be earlier said that this would be the time when fewer people are expecting the Lord. Thirty years ago, everybody was expecting the Lord and talking about it. Now, fewer are thinking, and fewer are talking about it. If you press people, they will admit that they believe in the second coming of Christ, but they are not looking for it expectantly. The last thing that bears upon the imperativeness of doing something about our spiritual life now is that we have such a short time to prepare is an act of moral folly. For anyone to have a day given to prepare, it is an act of inexcusable folly to let anything hinder that preparation. If we find ourselves in a spiritual rut, nothing in the world should hinder us. Nothing in this world is worth it. If we believe in eternity, if we believe in God, if we believe in the eternal existence of the soul, then there is nothing important enough to cause us to commit such an act of moral folly.[10]

Heaven is for prepared people, and a big part of that preparation is repentance. "We must repent of the sins of existing society, cast off the spell of the lies protecting our social wrongs, have faith in a higher social order, and realize in ourselves a new type of Christian [personhood] which seeks to overcome the evil in the present world, not by withdrawing from the world, but by revolutionizing it."[11]

---

10. Tozer Devotional/ Preparing Now for Then "The Alliance Tozer Devotional" Fri. June 05, 2020.
11. Walter Rauschenbusch, *Christianity And The Social Crisis* (New York: The MacMillan Company, 1907), 412.

Chapter Three

UNFAITHFUL STEWARD

> *And the day came when the risk to remain tight in a bud was more painful than the risk it took to blossom.* —Anais Nin

One of the worst things that makes the Lord angry is when we fail to take risks for the Kingdom of God. When we play it safe, as the postmodern church is doing today, we kindle the anger of the Lord because playing it safe means we have backed away from engaging in the battle for justice and the transformation of the world. This parable shows divine disfavor against buried talent that produces nothing, costs nothing, and gains nothing. How in the world will the church move from church militant to church triumphant when it is afraid to take risks? When Christians and non-Christians bury their voices and their actions against wrong, evil, and injustice, what value are they to the Kingdom of God? In the face of glaring racism, white supremacy, and the violence that theologically and politically justifies it, has the postmodern church buried the most important critical variable in life: social and economic justice? Like a hidden treasure, many Christians are complicit in keeping justice buried to keep others from finding it because they are afraid they may be killed for its enormous value. What is the reason to keep justice buried? Is it to only serve the rich and the well-connected while denying it to the poor and the oppressed of society? Why are Christians afraid to be controversial, afraid to be relevant for such a time as this? The future of America and the world are held in the balance against those who are risk-takers and those who are not. Severe punishment is waiting on those who have decided to play it safe and keep justice buried and the social order undisturbed.

The talents the Lord has given us are to engage the world, not run and hide from it. No war for justice and righteousness has ever been won in hiding. Nobody can offer solutions, right the wrongs, bring transformation, and create new possibilities unless they come out of their hiding places, anonymity, and apathy and make themselves visible to the Kingdom of God. It seems many Christians are buried behind the stain glass windows of their brick and mortar buildings, buried in ecclesiastical duties, buried in ministries that only minister to themselves, and staying within the lines of acceptable demarcation. Talents that could be put to use to gain souls and achieve justice for the Kingdom of God are buried within the confines of Christian communities. Like the Dead Sea, which has a high concentration of saltwater because it has no run off into other bodies of water and is forced to evaporate, so it is with the influence of Christians in society. Because too many Christians stay buried in their local churches, and there is no run off of their talents in society, the salt water of the Kingdom of God is forced to evaporate in a world that needs its healing power.

We wonder why there is a great falling away from Christianity and the church; too many Christians have practiced disengagement of the world, and the message of the Kingdom of God is evaporating in places where it should be flowing like a mighty stream. With the many wrongs and injustices growing in our nation and the world in geometric proportions, justice cannot wait! Martin Luther King, Jr stated. "For years now, I have heard the words "Wait!" . . . This "Wait" has almost always meant "Never." It has been a tranquilizing thalidomide, relieving the emotional stress for a moment, only to give birth to an ill-formed infant of frustration. We must come to see with the distinguished jurist of yesterday that 'justice too long delayed is justice denied."

Christians cannot wait for the right time to act to bring about justice because justice should be central to the socioeconomic life of any nation. There is no way we can have a relationship with God and offer up praise and worship to Him when justice is being tramped under the feet of society. The prophet Amos spoke about the interconnectedness of justice and worship. When one is denied, the other is inauthentic. God does not want to hear our prayers, our sermons, our songs, and accept our religious rituals when justice is peripheral and not central in the life of a nation. When justice is denied, God is saying to the nation, especially to the postmodern church in that nation, "I hate, I despise your religious festivals; your assemblies are a stench to me. Even though you bring me burnt offerings and grain offerings, I will not accept them. Though you bring choice fellowship offerings, I will have no regard for them. Away with the noise of your songs! I will not listen to the music of your harps. But let justice roll on like a river, righteousness like a never-failing stream (Amos 5:21-24)."

If justice is not part of the fabric of society, and or if justice is partial toward the rich and denied to the poor, it is an exercise in futility to hold worship services, national celebrations, religious conventions, revivals, and other rituals that invoke God. God repudiates all of it. We may take justice lightly, but it is the essence of who God is. Justice and righteousness are the twin towers of God's throne. When we refuse to stand up for justice, execute justice, and make justice impartial, we refuse the essence of God. When we refuse the essence of God, we undermine our liberties and existence. Thomas Jefferson said, "Can the liberties of a nation be thought secure when we have removed their only firm basis, a conviction in the minds of the people that these liberties are of the gift of God? That they are not to be violated but with his wrath? Indeed, I tremble for my country when I reflect that God is just: that his justice cannot sleep forever."[1]

Instead of taking the talents given to us to make justice a reality and increase the reign of God on earth, many Christians have buried them only to give back in return the same percentage they have been given. The noninvestment of justice and equality to engage the world in its transformation and we bury the opportunity carries an eternal penalty of condemnation. Think of how Black Americans have given their sweat, toil, tears, and lives for the progress and prosperity of America, but there is still no real economic and social justice investment from white America. In America, we are supposed to be a nation of laws, and our constitutional creed says, "We, the People of the United States, in order to form a more perfect Union, establish Justice, insure domestic Tranquility." We also have pledged to

---

1. Thomas Jefferson, *Notes on the State of Virginia*, Query XVIII: Manners, 1781.

be "One nation under God, indivisible, with liberty and justice for all." Every citizen of this nation is supposed to fall heir to this constitutional promise with the guarantee of liberty and justice for all. This is a check that no American should be denied of its constitutional funds. But, often, our creeds and our deeds don't match because the poor, the oppressed, and the marginalized often try to cash this check, but it keeps bouncing, saying "insufficient funds." It keeps bouncing for justice and equal treatment under the law; it keeps bouncing in the inner cities and urban areas of America. It keeps bouncing in the criminal justice system; it keeps bouncing in education; it keeps bouncing in the housing industry; it keeps bouncing in the courts. It keeps bouncing in our government. The check of justice, equality, and fair treatment keeps bouncing in many institutions of our society. Due to institutional racism in inner cities and urban areas, we have what Martin Luther King, Jr. called "The Other America."

> The other America and I use this title because there are literally two Americas. Every city in our country has this kind of dualism; this schizophrenia split into so many parts, and so every city ends up being two cities rather than one. There are two Americas. One America is beautiful . . . In this America, millions of people have the milk of prosperity and the honey of equality flowing before them. This America is the habitat of millions of people who have food and material necessities for their bodies, culture and education for their minds, freedom and human dignity for their spirits. In this America, children grow up in the sunlight of opportunity. But there is another America. This other America has a daily ugliness about it that transforms the buoyancy of hope into the fatigue of despair. In this other America, men walk the streets in search of jobs that do not exist . . . millions of people are forced to live in distressing housing conditions . . . thousands of young people are deprived of an opportunity to get an adequate education . . . thousands finish high school reading at a seventh, eighth, and sometimes ninth-grade level. Not because they're dumb, not because they don't have the native intelligence, but because the schools are so inadequate, so over-crowded, so devoid of quality, so segregated if you will, that the best in these minds can never come out. Probably the most critical problem in the

other America is economic. There are so many . . . who can never make ends meet because their incomes are far too low if they have incomes, and their jobs are so devoid of quality. And so, in this other America, unemployment is a reality . . . So the vast majority of negroes in America find themselves perishing on a lonely island of poverty in the midst of a vast ocean of material prosperity.[2]

Due to the ongoing oppression and racial injustice of black people, the economic non-investment of white America in black America, and in many ways black American in itself, furthers the dualism we find in many of our cities and states across the nation. William R. Jones furthers the argument King made about the two Americas.

The inner logic of oppression affirms a two-category system. It divides the human family into at least two distinct groups, hierarchically arranged into alleged superior and inferior classes . . . This hierarchical arrangement is correlated with a gross imbalance of power, access to life-extending and life-enhancing resources, and privileges. The alleged superior group will possess the unobscured surplus and the alleged inferior group, a grossly disproportionate deficit. To make the same point in different terms, the alleged superior group will have the most of whatever the society defines as the best and the least of the worst. In stark contrast, the alleged inferior group will have the least of the best and the most of the worst.[3]

Through this parable, the Lord has made it known that He will hold us accountable for the talents given to us. When He returns at an hour, we think not; we better be ready to show how we have put to good use the talents given to us and hope the Lord is pleased with what we have done with them. If we have made good on the talents given to us, we shall hear the words, "Well done, good and faithful servant! You have been faithful with a few things; I will put you in charge of many things. Come and share your Master's happiness (Matthew 25:23)." If we have buried or hidden

---

2. Martin Luther King, Jr., "The Other America," Speech given at Grosse Pointe High School on March 14, 1968.
3. William R. Jones, *Purpose and Method in Liberation Theology: Implication for an Interim Assessment*, in *Liberation Theology: North American Style*, edited by Deane William Ferm (New York: Verizon, 1987) 152–53.

the talents given us, which many Christians have done, we shall hear "You wicked, lazy servant! . . . Throw that worthless servant outside into the darkness, where there will be weeping and gnashing of teeth (Matthew 25:26, 30)." Outside into the darkness is believed to be hell or separation from God. Whatever its interpretation, it is not good. Once separated from God, souls are lost forever. Therefore, we must take seriously the talents given to us because there are eternal consequences on the day of reckoning for not putting into use what we have been given. "Is the point really to be productive? No, the point is to try something, anything that will benefit the master to some degree. The first and second servants were not equally productive, yet they received the same commendation and reward. The master was angry with the third servant for letting fear render him fruitless. He was unwilling to take any risk with what he had been given. It turns out this parable is not so much about stewardship and productivity as it is about taking risks for the master's benefit. That is what pleases the Lord."[4]

The principal of the parable is talents can represent a wide range of things, such as natural abilities, gifts, skills, opportunities, money, influence, etc. Those who invest their talents in advancing the kingdom of God will receive more responsibility and enter the joy of the Lord. Those who buried and did nothing with their talents, especially when they could have represented the two pillars of God's throne—justice and righteousness—will be harshly punished and banished from the Lord's sight forever. Too many people, especially Christians, don't take this responsibility seriously enough to be prepared for the great day of reckoning. "Human actions are of consequential importance, and we cannot be responsible for those consequences, for this is an essential prerequisite for human freedom.[5] People not only bury their talents, but many more squander their talents in a world that doesn't glorify God or advance God's Kingdom.

Many started in the church, where their gifts and talents edified believers, but they soon allowed the world to siphon off their talents to the world. Once they are siphoned off to the world, they get caught up in fame and fortune with their addictions and end up spiritually defeated and destroyed. They obtained material success but ended spiritual failures. They

---

4. Doug Newton, *Fresh Eyes On Jesus' Parables* (David C Cook, Publisher, 2018), 173–74.
5. Chris Marshall, *The Little Book Of Biblical Justice* (Intercourse, PA: Good Books Publisher, 2005), 19.

didn't understand or believe what Jesus said, "What shall it profit a man if he gains the whole world, and loses his soul (Mark 8:36)?" Charles Thomas Studd reminds us, "Only one life, yes only one, soon will its fleeting hours be done; then, in 'that day' my Lord to meet, and stand before His judgment seat; only one life,' twill soon be past, only what's done for Christ will last."[6] Jesus Christ does not want us to allow anybody or anything to get in the way of our relationship with Him, no matter how much we are offered for our talents. We are given talents to help advance the Kingdom of God, not the Kingdom of this world. The entering of lost souls into the Kingdom of God is the spiritual profit for investing our talents, and we who have done this will enter into the joy of the Lord.

For this reason, the Lord does not want us to bury our talents and opportunities for the benefit of the Kingdom of God. He wants us to let our light shine before the world so that they may see our good works and glorify the Father, who is in heaven (Matthew 5:16). Notice here our talents should be used for good works to glorify God, not ourselves nor the world. Buried talents cannot be seen nor produce good works. No excuse will be accepted on the day of reckoning for buried talents. Buried talents that could have made a difference in the world could have transformed situations that could have corrected oppression, brought justice to the poor and orphans that could have relieved suffering by providing housing for the homeless, feeding the hungry, clothing the naked, providing education for the disadvantaged; that could have created opportunities for the downtrodden; that could have brought peace to a world torn by war; that could have been the leaven in the body politic of the nation transforming policies that affect people lives—certainly will generate outrage from the Lord who will not spare during the day of judgment.

The Lord invested these talents in us to bring God's governance to a world wrought by sin and evil. These talents given to us have nothing to do with the color of our skin or our socio-economic standing. We all will be held accountable for the investment the Lord has made in us, and it will be dreadful to hear the words, "Wicked and lazy servant!" What God has entrusted to us could have made all the difference in the world had we put

---

6. Cited from Wyatt, Cindy, "Only One Life, Twill Soon Be Past," poem by Charles Thomas Studd, Poetry About Jesus and Salvation, retrieved 13 September 2013.

these talents to work. But, because of fear, many people did not take the risk and use their talents triggering the angry response of the Lord. A little return on God's investment is better than no return. Therefore, the Lord's anger will be poured out against "wicked and lazy servants" by ordering them to be cast out into utter darkness.

Why much anger and harsh words from the Lord? As Myles Munroe stated, "The wealthiest place in the world is not the gold mines of South America or the oil fields of Iraq or Iran. They are not the diamond mines of South Africa or the banks of the world. The wealthiest place on the planet is just down the road. It is the cemetery. There lie buried companies that were never started, inventions that were never made, bestselling books that were never written, and masterpieces that were never painted. In the cemetery is buried the greatest treasure of untapped potential."[7] They took their talents to the grave, robbing the Kingdom of God of what they could have contributed and gotten in return. Think of all the people who could have made a difference but didn't; who could have saved lives; who could have transformed society; who could have eliminated hunger; who could have revolutionized education, medicine, economies, and governments, and brought humanity closer to the Kingdom of God on earth but did not.

The fact that people took their talents to the grave, the graveyard is the richest place on planet earth. We will never know how much impact they could have made on the world. But, due to the fact, they were fearful of investing their talents, they robbed themselves and humanity of solutions that could have set the world on a new trajectory that could have ended nuclear proliferation that could have saved untold numbers of children and a host of other international woes that keep humanity on the proverbial edge. It is eternally dangerous and deadly to bury the talents the Lord has given us. "When God gives you a seed, He doesn't want that seed back; He wants a forest. He wants you to plant and grow that seed with the ability He gave you. When God gives you something, it always contains more than is apparent. His seeds have the potential to become more than what initially appears. He gives you His seed of potential with the end product in it, and it is the end product—not the seed—that God wants back."[8]

---

7. Myles Monroe, Quotes, www.goodreads.com.
8. Myles Munroe, *The Burden of Freedom* (Lake Mary, FL: Charisma House, 2000, 2001), 173.

Just think, if Frederick Douglass and the abolitionists had buried their talents, America would be much worse today. Just think, if Abraham Lincoln buried his talents, our land would be less free today. Just think, if the Wright brothers had buried their talents, we wouldn't have airplanes today. Just think, if Henry Ford had buried his talents, we wouldn't have automobiles today. Just think, if Garrett M. Morgan had buried his talents, we wouldn't have traffic lights today. Just think, if George Washington Carver had buried his talents, we wouldn't have many of the products he discovered from two peanuts. Just think, if Steve Jobs had buried his talents, we wouldn't have all the apple products that have transformed the world of technology. What if Martin Luther King, Jr. had buried his talents? We probably wouldn't have civil and voting rights today. What if Madam CJ Walker, Rosie Parks, Mary McCloud Bethune, and other known and unknown women buried their talents? We wouldn't have progressed in the areas of science, education, economics, social justice, children protection and national alerts. Just think, if I had buried this book from being written, it would deprive readers of doing better and motivating them to get in a hurry to meet the Lord. Whenever we refuse to share our talents, we deprive families, communities, the church, the nation, and the world of what the Lord has given us. God did not give us talents to bury them but to use them to make a difference in this world.

Too many people have buried their talents in excuses, in anger, in resentment, in complacency, in apathy, in hurt feelings, in selfishness, in egoism, in jealousy and envy, in mixed-up priorities, refusing to use them to move the world, the nation, and the church to a better place. We are no good to anybody when we bury our talents. Jesus Christ wants us to use what He has given us. To be faithful stewards, we don't need a Ph.D. or a master's degree; we don't need to know Socrates' philosophy; we don't need to know Plato's symposium; we don't need to know Aristotle's syllogisms; we don't need to know Einstein's theory of relativity. All we need is a heart full of the Holy Spirit and a willing mind to serve the Lord by using our talents that make a lasting change in this world.[9] The world awaits our talents, and through them, the Lord can reach a world that doesn't know

---

9. Paraphrased from Martin Luther King, Jr. last sermon, "Drum Major Instinct," Ebenezer Baptist Church, February 4, 1968.

Him or what He has done for mankind. Our talents are our Kingdom seeds, and since we are sowers in this world, it is incumbent upon us to plant the seeds of the Kingdom of God through our talents.

In the parable of the talents, the servant who was given one talent, which represents many people, stood before the Lord only to give back what he had been given. The servant made no effort to invest what he had; he was spiritually lazy and unproductive. The excuse he used was, "Lord, I knew you were a hard man, reaping where you have not sown, gathering where you have not scattered seed. And I was afraid and went and hid your talent in the ground. Look, there you have what is yours." The Lord's response was simply this: no investment, no return, equals no entrance into the Kingdom of God. How often do people make excuses for not investing their talents for the gain of the Kingdom of God? People use "isms" as an excuse not to invest their talents. They use racism, sexism, sectarianism, denominationalism, and other "isms." Not that "isms" aren't legitimate concerns and do hinder people from life opportunities, but people should not allow themselves to make excuses for not investing their talents despite the "isms" of opposition. But, instead of people investing their talents, they make excuses for being either fearful, lazy, or irresponsible.

The Lord said to the servant who buried his talent, "You wicked and lazy servant, you knew that I reap where I have not sown and gather where I have not scattered seed. So you ought to have deposited my money with the bankers, and at my coming, I would have received back my own with interest. So take the talent from him, and give it to him who has ten talents . . . and cast the unprofitable servant into utter darkness." This servant's return was death for trying to give back the same seed given to him. Judgment was brought on this servant because he could have made a difference; he could have gotten a return on the one talent, but he buried it. He blew the opportunity to at least gain some interest. People don't know that the little they have makes a big difference.

How would you feel if someone had the skills to save children from a deadly disease but refused to use the skills, and these children unnecessarily died? How would you feel if someone had resources that could have been invested to benefit the whole community, but the resources were wasted? How would you feel if your local church could have kept its doors open but the church closed because the members refused to invest resources in the ministry? How would you feel if a farmer could have fed thousands of people but refused to invest the seed in the soil? How would you feel if someone knew CPR and refused to practice it on someone, and that person died as a result? How would you feel if justice could have been given to a person, and it was denied and caused a riot in which people and property were lost? This is the reason the Lord is angry with this servant and likewise with the church, America and the nations of the world. There is no excuse for homelessness, poverty, and the denial of universal health care. Leaders who play politics put party over principle and allow people to suffer and die will hear the Savior say, "Cast [these] unprofitable servants into utter darkness." Those who get rich from unjust policies while the poor and the needy go without their basic needs being met will hear the words, "Cast [these] unprofitable servants into utter darkness." Those who could have made a difference socially, economically, educationally, medically, politically, and spiritually but refused to do so will hear the words, "Cast [these] unprofitable servants into utter darkness." The Lord wants a return on what he has given us, and if we return to the Lord exactly what He has given us with no addition or profit, and the Lord doesn't punish us, then the Lord owes an apology to the servant in the parable.

    The servant buried his talent because he was suffering from a disease called "giveupitis." He gave up before he started. He didn't want to take a risk. All investment entails some risk, and if we are afraid to be risk-takers for the Kingdom of God, our stewardship will be found wanting. The reason so many people, communities, and churches are stuck where they are, they are afraid to take risks. They are afraid the landscape may change; they are afraid they may lose control; they are afraid more work may be required of them; they are afraid of failure, and believe it or not, some people are afraid of success. Like the children of Israel, people would rather go back and suffer in the same places the Lord is trying to bring them out. They would prefer the thorns and thickets of the wilderness than take risks for the Promised Land. They would rather hold captive a church, a community, and a nation because they are afraid to take risks. Risk-taking is what productivity is made of. If we never take risks, we can never move ahead. If we never take risks, we can never be productive, never be relevant, never be free, and never please God through Christ because faith is risk-taking.

Moses took a risk when he stretched out his rod over the Red Sea. Joshua and the children of Israel took a risk when they marched around the Jericho Wall. David took a risk when he stood before the giant Goliath. Daniel took a risk when he refused to stop praying. The three Hebrew young men took a risk when they refused to bow before the idol god. Jesus took a risk when he took two fishes and five barley loads of bread and fed five thousand. Abraham Lincoln took a risk when he signed the Emancipation Proclamation. Harriet Tubman took a risk when she led 300 slaves to freedom. Thurgood Marshal took a risk when he argued against segregation before the Supreme Court. President L.B. Johnson took a risk when he signed the Civil Rights and Voting Rights bills of the 1960s. At the end of the 1960s, American astronauts risk their lives to go to the moon. It was a giant and successful step for mankind. There are examples after examples of people taking risks and having enormous results. We must learn how to take risks if we are to advance the Kingdom of God.

How is it that we can risk going to the moon but cannot risk correcting social and economic injustices to make democracy a complete reality for all Americans? How is it that we can have money for incarceration but little to no money for education? "We have achieved electric lights, but they have not lighted the way to justice and brotherhood. We have mastered refrigeration but it has not cooled the angry passions of man's heart. We have built towering skyscrapers, but they have brought us no nearer to God. We have achieved giant power, but never has been powerful enough to save a single man from his inner evil."[10] Until we learn to take risks in areas that really improve human relations, justice, and equality for all God's people, other costly risks won't save us. Many of the solutions to our national and international problems are buried under racism, sexism, hedonism, sectarianism, and militarism. If given a chance to come out from among these "isms" we just may forge another world where justice, peace, and brotherhood are the order of the day. But, as long as we continue to bury the values that matter for democracy and the Kingdom of God, we will never know what could have been. America is a great country only by

---

10. Harry Emerson Fosdick, *Answers To Real Problems*, edited by Mark E. Yurs, 135.

force. What if she became great by love, justice, equality, and those things the nation often keeps buried but are necessary for her continued existence without fear? Jesus Christ won't look favorably on people and nations that buried their talents that could have radically made a difference.

The question is, what have we buried? Whatever we have buried we better get in a hurry and put it to use because the return of Jesus Christ is upon us. Some people have buried love, justice, and equality; some have buried courage; others righteous indignation; some forgiveness; some public witness, others goodness, gentleness and self-control; some cooperation, participation, unity, resources, leadership, and much-needed evangelism. Whatever we have buried that could assist in freeing people, making the world more just and humane, and adding souls to the Kingdom of God won't go unpunished. It could cost people their eternal life with the Lord. Therefore, the frantic plea to us all is don't let the Lord catch us with our work undone. The punishment is nonreversible.

Chapter Four

BANNED FROM THE BANQUET

> *My life has become extremely hard. I am banned on Twitter. I'm banned on Uber. I'm banned on Lyft. I'm banned on Venmo. I'm banned on GoFundMe. I'm banned on PayPal. I'm banned on Uber Eats.* —Laura Loomer

We are living in times in which problems that could be solved are not; improvements that could be made aren't; a transformation that could happen doesn't; divisions that could be bridged are not because people have become habitual excuse-makers. Excuses have become part of the social, economic, religious, and political fabric of our country and the world; it is rooted in our collective will to explain away what we refuse to do. The ontological excuses we make on a daily basis only push our nation, the church, and the world to the brink of ruin. Nations that have made excuses in the past for not taking responsibility and doing what is right, just, and godly are now in the junk heap of history. Rudyard Kipling said, "We have forty million reasons for failure, but not a single excuse. So the more we work and the less we talk, the better results we shall get—We have had an Imperial lesson; it may make us an Empire yet!"[1] America is now a powerful empire similar to the Roman Empire, and we continue making millions

---

1. Rudyard Kipling's, *American Notes* (A Word to the Wise, Publisher), August 6, 2013.

of excuses for our failure to be an authentic democracy, to be a just and humane nation, to provide a living wage for the working class, to invest in quality education for all children; to provide health care for all citizens, to reform the criminal justice system, to deal with climate change issues; to correct ecological waste in communities of color and a host of other solvable issues facing this country. There is no doubt unless America confronts and corrects her national problems, she too shall fall like the Roman Empire. Too many people, too many leaders, and too many Christians are failing to do justly, love mercy, and walk humbly with God. Wealth and power won't destroy America; injustice will. To continue making excuses won't make our society, our nation, and the world better. Those who stand on the sideline, who continue busy as usual, and who are in denial about the social and economic racial injustice are just as much a part of the demise of the nation as those who are outright working against it.

Excuses have become endemic in the American culture. Local, state, and national leaders are making excuses. Schools are making excuses. Parents are making excuses. Young people are making excuses. Churches are making excuses. It seems that every institution that holds this nation together is making excuses for its demise. We are blaming each other and have become a nation of excuse-makers. What can get done is not; what is possible to change is unchanged, not because we don't have the resources, not because we don't have the skills; we fail to have the will. We have put power above principle, money above morality, demagoguery above democracy, and injustice above justice. As long as American Christians continue to support policies against the poor and the least of these and make excuses for it, the nation can never become the more perfect union she espouses to be. It is inexcusable to cut the federal budget against the most vulnerable of society. It is unpardonable before the Lord who made the poor, the outcast, the left out, and the marginalized his top priority, and America puts them on the back burner of national concern if they are on the burner of concern at all. Our health care should not be a privilege; it should be a right for all citizens. Just like prayer is not a privilege, it is a right of all God's children to make their request known to the Lord. But, America is offering excuses for making the rich richer and the poor poorer, using God and unchecked capitalism as the cover for this continued practice.

When we see widespread use of drugs, rampant teenage pregnancy, rising high-school dropouts, crippling illiteracy, crime in high and low places, the break down of the family, gun violence across the nation, police killings of people of color, political division, and a host of other solvable problems, we are making excuses why these problems continue to exist. What is more troubling is many Christians are making excuses for not obeying the gospel by aggressively challenging the government to "Let justice roll down like water and righteousness like a mighty stream." The Gospel of Jesus Christ is good news to the poor, the vulnerable, and the marginalized of society. Christians cannot get around putting in action the words of Jesus as the starting point of ministry: "The Spirit of the LORD is upon Me, Because He has anointed Me To preach the gospel to the poor; He has sent Me to heal the brokenhearted, To proclaim liberty to the captives And recovery of sight to the blind, To set at liberty those who are oppressed (Luke 4:18)." Any Christian and church that never mentions the suffering of the poor due to structural injustice should understand why there is a hermeneutics of suspicion of where their loyalty lies. We cannot preach about the life of Christ and overlook the vulnerable of society.

James Cone stated, "To believe in the Gospel means creating solidarity with the oppressed. Jesus' cross is God's solidarity with the weak and the lost. When we follow Jesus into the ghetto, it always creates conflict in a racially divided society. White theologians do not speak out against white supremacy because such speaking will surely make them unpopular in their group. Of all the evils that exist in society, racism is one of the most intractable because it is so difficult to name and so easy to deny."[2] Christians who never mention the suffering of others make religion an opiate, the gospel irrelevant and preach empty platitudes. We have made excuses for so long about not applying the Gospel of Jesus Christ to the everyday lives of suffering people; we have learned to lie to ourselves and pass the lie on to others.

Too many Christians replace prayer for action instead of using prayer as a motivator to act against institutional injustices that create what Martin Luther King, Jr. called "An edifice of beggars." King said, "True compassion

---

2. James H. Cone, "Theologians and White Supremacy: An interview with James H. Cone," americamagazine.org, November 20, 2006.

is more than flinging a coin to a beggar; it is not haphazard and superficial. It comes to see that an edifice that produces beggars needs restructuring. A true revolution of values will soon look uneasily on the glaring contrast of poverty and wealth . . . and say: This is not just."[3] The socioeconomic edifice that was predicated upon black oppression has never undergone restructuring. For 401 years, the American system has oppressed, maligned, mistreated, marginalized, dehumanized, and exploited black people. Some changes have been made, but corrections have been suppressed. As stated in my earlier writings, change doesn't necessarily mean you have a correction. When a house has structural problems with cracks in the foundation, and all we do is paint over the cracks, we have made a change, but we have not corrected the problem. Until the cracks are sealed and the foundation is made sure, we have only made changes that aren't corrections.

Those who argue that black America should change their behavior and take responsibility for their lives are partially true, but even when blacks do this, they still are operating within the system of injustice. They are not participating in power to correct the system that works against them. Until the socioeconomic system is corrected, good behavior won't achieve justice. All we are doing is acting like a pelican stuck in the mud. Once the pelican sticks his beck in the mud, he gets his feet out; then his beck is stuck; then he puts his feet back in the mud to get his beck out, only to have his feet stuck again in the mud. Until we correct racism and oppression, we are stuck in the mud of an unjust system. We must figure out how to get out of the socioeconomic mud of our situation and restructure society in such a way that eliminates structural injustice. We can do it if we ontologically will it! Just as we ontologically, scientifically, and economically figured out how to go to the moon, we can figure out how to restructure our socioeconomic system to be just and fair to all people who live in America. Again, it can be achieved, but it's going to take our collective will and determination more than our collective prayers.

Now, I believe in prayer. But as it is said, "Prayer is a brave man's hope and not a coward's excuse." Many Christians pray and send God everywhere. I hear many say, "Lord, go to the schools; Lord, go to the prisons; Lord, go to the orphanages; Lord, go to that family down the street that is in need.

---

3. Martin Luther King, Jr., *"A Time to Break Silence,"* Riverside Church, New York City, April 4, 1967.

Lord, clean up our neighborhoods. Lord, hold our politicians accountable. Lord, raise our children; Lord, talk to our youth. Lord, stop the violence in our communities. Lord, get rid of racism and transform our American system." We treat the Lord like an almighty bellhop, sending Him to places where we ought to be going and asking Him to do for us what we ought to be doing for ourselves. Frederick Douglass said, "It seems to me that the true philosophy of reform is not found in the clouds, or in the stars, or anywhere else outside of humanity itself. So far as the laws of the universe have been discovered and understood, they seem to teach that the mission of man's improvement and perfection has been wholly committed to man himself. So, is he to be his own savior or his own destroyer? He has neither angels to help him nor devils to hinder him."[4] The transformation of the world is in the hands of mankind, and unless we take action to correct the wrong, wrong will go unchallenged and uncorrected.

Theologian and philosopher William R. Jones believes transformation can only occur when we become ultimate agents in human history and take responsibility for our God-given freedom. We cannot expect God to do the transformative work in the world while we do not do our part. We must join God in the process of transformation. Jones calls it "humanocentric theism," the process of God and humans working together. When both humans and God collaborate, the possibility exists to correct oppression and restructure society so justice can be central in the life of the nation. The possibility remains within the oppressive context as long as the collaboration covenant is faithful to its agreement. But, when we humans break the collaboration covenant, we nullify God's participation in the process of transformation. Jones said, "Thus God's responsibility for the crimes and errors of human history is reduced if not effectively eliminated."[5] When we decide not to include God in the affairs of humanity, we cannot blame God for oppression, racism, inequality, and all the crimes of human history, no matter how often we invoke His name. Under the law in which God created humans, God respects the decisions of humans even when it means we don't join God in the transformation of the world. In freedom,

---

4. *The Frederick Douglass Papers,* "It Moves," Washington: Library of Congress, 1976 (Manuscript Division, Microfilm 28:18).

5. William R. Jones, *Is God A White Racists?* (New York: Double Day Anchor, 1973), xxii.

we can lead the world to redemption or perdition. "Humanocentric theism" is when we are God's hands and feet in the struggle for justice.

God is not our Jennie in a bottle; God is not a rabbit's foot or a good luck charm. God is not our servant; we are His servants, and in the places we send God, God is already there. God needs some hands, some feet, some eyes, and some tongues to work through. Chris Marshall said, "Present injustices must never simply be tolerated or accepted as inevitable. We are not meant to resign ourselves to the evils of the world while waiting passively for God's coming to sweep them away. Instead, we are to work tirelessly in partnership with God for the greater attainment of justice here and now, knowing that God shall ultimately bring our efforts to fruition in the renewal of creation. God's coming justice is the culmination of, not a substitute for, human striving for greater justice here and now."[6] To achieve a just society, we must cooperate with God through Jesus Christ, and this can only happen within the context of obedience. "Obedience to God means seeking to do God's will that embodies trusting cooperation with Him. Good outcomes are produced by God and the believer acting together; they work in cooperation with each other; human participation is required for the divine purpose. The believer may not see the goal(s) at the beginning of the process of working with God. But during its course, the believer becomes aware of the goal best suited to herself. Of course, faith may fail at times, as when Peter walked on the water to come to Jesus (Mt 14:28-33), but like Peter, God intervenes to save people from doubt and wrong decisions. Cooperation with God is only half of the equation, however, for God triune also wants people to love each other as oneself, to assist and cooperate with each other."[7]

But, we make excuses for disobedience to God because we don't want to cooperate with God or with one another. Our noncooperation with God and one another is leading to our demise. When we don't hold leaders and people accountable for their behavior, our democracy is weakened and our national and international reputation wanes. Erwin W. Lutzer stated, "If we keep Christ to ourselves out of fear of reprisals, are we not taking our stand with those pastors in Germany who chose to close ranks with

---

6. Chris Marshall, *The Little Book of Biblical Justice*, 29.
7. Beed, Clive, and Cara Beed. "Jesus on Cooperation." *Transformation*, vol. 32, no. 2, 2015, 99–111. JSTR, www.jstor.org/stable/90010968, accessed 8 Jan. 2021.

Hitler? Is not our sin even greater since the consequences of our obedience to Christ are so minimal in comparison with what they faced? Are we qualified to sit in judgment of the church in Germany if we have never lost a job or failed a course because we are Christians?"[8]

As long as we leave reform to chance and look to God to straighten out the mess we allowed to happen, the future looks darker than it is today. Mankind is still finding ways to destroy himself, his community, his nation, and the world. Too many Christians want a crown but make excuses for not picking up their cross. They want crops but make excuses for not plowing up the ground; they want a growing church but make excuses for not changing their methods. They want baptism but make excuses for no church disciple; they want grace but make excuses for cheap grace; grace without repentance; grace without responsibility; and grace without Jesus Christ. The world is in a spiritual crisis, and Christians are making excuses for the crisis. The following poem describes why the world remains untransformed. It is called: Excuses, excuses, you hear them everyday.

Now, the devil he'll supply them if from church you stay away. When people come to know the Lord, the devil always loses. So, to keep them folks away from church, he offers them excuses!

> In the summer, it's too hot, and in the winter, it's too cold. And in the springtime, when the weather's just right, You find some places else to go. Well, it's up to the mountain or down to the beach or to visit some old friend, or just stay at home and kinda relax and hope some of the kinfolks drop in.
>
> Well, the church bench is too hard, and that choir sings way too loud. And, boy, you know how nervous you can get when you setting in a great big crowd.
>
> The doctor told you you'd better watch them crowds, they'll set you back, but you go to that ballgame, 'cause you say it helps you to relax.
>
> The preacher, he's too young, maybe he's too old. His sermons, they're not fired enough, or maybe they're too bold. His voice is much too quiet, sometimes he gets too loud, he needs to have more dignity or else he's way too proud.

---

8. Erwin W. Lutzer, *When A Nation Forgets God* (Chicago: Moody Publishers, 2010), 120.

His sermons, they're too long. Maybe, they're too short.
He ought to preach the Word with dignity, instead of stomp and snort. Why, one of the members told me the other day, "He didn't even shake my hand." So, I will stay away [as much as I can].[9]

Jesus makes it abundantly clear that those who make excuses will be banned from the banquet. They will not enjoy eternal fellowship with Christ, who is the author and finisher of our faith. Jesus tells the parable of the wedding banquet that we might reorder our priorities. For many Christians, Jesus is so low on their agenda He has really become irrelevant. Many Christians are so busy with the cares of this world that they don't have time for fellowship with Jesus Christ. No fellowship, no discipleship. Christ does not fit into the equation of many Christians' newfound success until something comes along that threatens their health and livelihood. Do they think about Jesus Christ, and that is only what He can do for them to restore what they have lost. Once they regain their health and livelihood, they go back to their previous agendas, of which Jesus Christ is left out. They once again become too busy for spiritual faithfulness.

There is not much excitement and glamour in spiritual things. People want to be where the crowd clings. Although Jesus warned people that the broad way leads to death, hell, and destruction, they still refuse to follow him and make excuses for not joining in the work of the Kingdom of God. In the parable when the banquet preparation is done, the Lord sends out his servant to tell the invited ones that everything is now ready. Come on in! The servant calls the invited guess to come, but one by one, they make excuses. Their matters were more important than fellowship with Jesus Christ. One made the excuse that he had bought a piece of land, and he must go and see it. The other makes the excuse that he had bought five yoke of oxen and he must go and inspect them. Another made the excuse that he had just married; therefore, he cannot come (Luke 14:15-24).

These excuses are no different than the excuses people make today. As a nation, we are still making excuses for hunger, homelessness, racial injustice, inequality, uninsured, and a host of other solvable problems.

---

9. "Excuses Lyrics." Lyrics.com. STANDS4 LLC, 2021. Web. 26 Mar. 2021. https://www.lyrics.com/lyric/5293481/William+Topley.

Jesus wants us to know that life in this world is transitory, and so are the benefits of our self-indulging investments transitory. The psalmist said, "Teach us to number our days, that we may apply our hearts unto wisdom (Psalms 90:12)." These invited guests in the parable made excuses, as many Christians are making today, and forfeiting their souls for short-term satisfaction. How are we going to know Christ, make him known, and make disciples, except we fellowship with Christ? Christians cannot make Him known when they don't know Him. When the servant came and told the Lord about the invited guess refusal to come, the Lord became angry. The Lord had spent a great deal of time and energy preparing the banquet. The Lord had given up so much in order that mankind might receive life. He became poor that we might become rich; he became our grief that we might have joy; he became our humiliation that we might have justification and glorification. Yet even today, many people refuse to come while making excuses. Therefore, Jesus told his servant to go out and invite the poor, the maimed, the halt, and the blind. Those who have been neglected, marginalized, oppressed, left out, poor, and rejected all are invited to come, and yet there is still room at the banquet. Those who made excuses and turned down the invitation to the banquet, Jesus said, "They will not taste of my banquet." They will not have eternal life. They are banned from the fellowship with Christ. To those who make excuses, there is an eschatological compensation of condemnation for people who choose this world over divine invitation. The late great Billy Graham said these words:

> Jesus tells this story to show that we cannot escape God's invitation. We have to say "yes, " or we have to say "no." Which will it be for you? . . . Some people say, "I am afraid of what others will think." That is one of the biggest excuses—peer pressure. The truth should determine our decision, not the crowd. I agree that it is difficult to be a follower of Christ, and part of the difficulty is that others may not agree with us. There were many in Jesus' day in the same situation. "For they loved the praise of men more than the praise of God," said Jesus. (John 12:43). Other people say, "If I come to Christ, there is too much to give up. I just can't do it." Yet, to buy something, we will work night and day, and we will give up family joys and comforts to labor overtime to earn

more. In search of health we will give up many precious privileges. We give up our favorite delicacies to lose weight. In search of athletic honor, Olympic athletes practice eight or ten hours a day for years. God accepts no excuse because you have heard the Gospel. He offers you an invitation to his feast."[10]

To join Christ at the eternal banquet, can American Christians give up their racism, their silence, their sideline spectatorship, and their complicity in wrong, evil, and injustice? If American Christians cannot give up these things and others, then think about this question, Jesus challenges us all with. "For what shall it profit a man (a woman, a church, a political party, a nation) if he shall gain the whole world and lose his own soul? Or what shall a man give in exchange for his soul (Mark 8:36-37)?" However way we answer says we will honor the invitation by following Christ or make excuses and lose our souls.

---

10. Billy Graham, "*Excuses God Won't Accept,*" Bible Faith Mission India Ministry, Source: Decision-September, 1982.

Chapter Five
NEGLECT BRINGS ETERNAL REGRET

Indifference and neglect often do much more damage than outright dislike. —J.K. ROWLING

There is nothing like seeing people hungry and cannot get enough to eat. It breaks the heart to witness the future of a nation that has children, and they are suffering from hunger that affects their physical, social, and intellectual development. Hunger, at least in America, is one social ill that should not be occurring in one of the greatest economies in the world. The basic needs of having a roof over our heads and food to eat are two necessities that people should not go without. Something is morally and critically wrong in a nation that allows such neglect to happen within its shores. This social injustice is so disturbing that divine outrage is poured upon nations that allow it to exist. There is no human rationalization that can ever excuse the deterioration of human creation due to malnutrition. Nations that have rich economies and do nothing to eliminate hunger and homelessness within their shores are waiting to be thrown onto the junk heap of history where beached bones of other nations are gathered. Any nation that neglects the hungry and the homeless has lost its soul, and eternal damnation is its final destination. Although hunger is not new, we have the resources and capability to eradicate it among us.

Neglect Brings Eternal Regret

Years ago, in 1987, when I was a student at Incarnate Word College in San Antonio, Texas, I submitted an essay and was fortunate to be picked among others across the nation to work with a grass-roots organization called Bread for the World in Washington, D.C. The purpose of Bread for the World is to keep the issue of hunger, both foreign and domestic, before Congress. I was there for ten weeks, hobnobbing with representatives and senators, trying to get funds to help the poor and needy. I lobbied for an increase in funds for a supplemental food assistance program called WIC (Women, Infants, and Children). While there in D.C. I also had a chance to visit the White House to see some of the luxurious rooms with their splendid furnishings. I walked across oriental rugs costing thousands of dollars; I saw million-dollar chandeliers hanging from the rafters of the White House. Everything about this house is extremely expensive, and I wondered what the president would have for dinner. Would it be a fresh Maine lobster? Would it be a six-inch T-bone steak taken from a southern-bred steer, or would he have a succulent rack of lamb? Whatever the menu, the president and the White House staff will eat well, and there is no gainsaying in the fact that whatever they wanted it would be at their disposal. They had plenty and then some to spare.

Continuing my tour, I walked outside of the White House and saw something that mortified me. Across from the White House in the park, I saw men, women, and children who where hungry and homeless; they were sleeping on benches; some had card board boxes as the only shelter over their heads, and others were asking for alms to get some bread to get them over another day. Observing from the White House, these poor and hungry people were invisible because the White House staff refused to see them. These people were in deep destitution and need of life-sustaining assistance. I could imagine them crying out with Ralph Ellison:

> I am an invisible man; I am a man of substance,
> of flesh and bone, fiber and liquids—and I might
> even be said to possess a mind. I am invisible
> understand, simply because people refuse to see me.[1]

---

1. Ralph Ellison, *Invisible Man,* Vintage Books, 2nd edition, Prologue, 1995.

I imagined them saying with Paul Laurence Dunbar, the great African American poet:

> A crust of bread and a corner to sleep in,
> A minute to smile and an hour to weep in,
> A pint of joy to a peck of trouble,
> And never a laugh but the moans come double;
> And that is life![2]

These people were overlooked, forgotten about, and made invisible because others refused to see them. These destitute people were right in plain sight of one of the richest houses in the world, yet they were invisible. How often do we refuse to see others in need? How often do we set our gaze on achieving other things but neglect to see what really matters in life? People matter! If it were not for the people, a lot of what we have and enjoy in life would not exist. Therefore, when people fall on hard times, we should not abandon them but give them a hand up until they are are to stand up again. Unfortunately, our highways and byways cause us to drive around the poor, the needy, slums and ghettos of our cities. It's a convenient way to divorce from the concerns and needs of inner-city people who are doing their best to keep food on the table. The poor and hungry of our cities are the results of benign neglect of government and other social institutions to commit to eradicating social structures that promote the marginalization of the poor and those who are suffering and going to bed hungry.

Hunger and homelessness are not new. The world has known about this phenomenon for millennia. But what is new is hunger and homelessness are no longer unsolvable problems. We have the technology and the resources to get rid of this social shame. What we lack is the will to do it. Arthur Simon said, "We have the capability to eliminate hunger, but we lack the will to do it. I do not say merely the will, because there is nothing mere about it. The will is more crucial and more stubbornly evasive than the necessary technology. And the will must not only be expressed in millions of individual efforts but translated into national policy decisions as well."[3]

---

2. Paul Laurence Dunbar, *The Complete Poems of Paul Laurence Dunbar* (CreateSpace Independent Publishing, 2018).

3. Arthur Simon, *Christian Faith & Public Policy No Grounds For Divorce* (Grand Rapids, MI: William B. Eerdmans Publishing Company, 1987), 44.

There are over 821 million hungry people in the world, and 35 million live here in the United States. "New evidence continues to signal that the number of hungry people in the world is growing, reaching 821 million in 2017 or one in every nine people, according to The State of Food Security and Nutrition in the World 2018 released today."[4] It is a shame before God that America has not made hunger and homelessness a major priority on its national agenda. The military budget has gone up significantly in the billions, while funds to get rid of hunger and homelessness have gone down dramatically. This senselessness prompted President Dwight Eisenhower to say once, "Every gun that is made, every warship launched, every rocket fired signifies, in the final sense, a theft from those who hunger and are not fed, those who cold and not clothed."[5] Not only has America failed in eradicating hunger and homelessness, but the postmodern church has failed also. The government and the church must partner to resolve this nagging issue. "This lack of political will presents a great challenge to U.S. Christians. We can use the gift of citizenship to help get our national leaders to make decisions that can turn an effort against hunger into a national commitment."[6] Hunger in our communities cannot be solved by a few words at the end of a prayer but by the first order of business on our ecclesiastical and political agenda. Because we refuse to see the poor, the hungry, and the destitute, those who are the direct objects of God's greatest concern in human society, the anger of the Lord is aroused, and no nation is safe.

Many people may think that hunger and homelessness are the results of laziness. This may be the case for a few people, but the great majority of people who are poor and hungry are a result of structural injustice that favors the rich over the poor. The great majority of people want to work, and many of them work at two or three jobs just to make ends meet. The issue is not necessarily having a job(s) but the justice of receiving just wages for the work that is done. When the cost of living out runs the compensation people receive for working, we cannot blame people for this imbalance. Laziness has nothing to do with how this imbalance of wages and the cost of living creates poverty, hunger, and homelessness. The issue is an unjust

---

4. Fadela Chaib, World Health Organization, "Global Hunger Continues to Rise, new UN report Says," September 11, 2018.

5. Dwight D. Eisenhower, "The Chance for Peace," an address before the American Society of Newspaper Editors on April 16, 1953.

6. Arthur Simon, *Christian Faith & Public Policy*, 45.

system that needs correcting, and when we don't have the will to correct an unjust social and economic system, we have no moral authority by equating wealth and work. It is not the will of God that one percent of people at the top hold more wealth than the combined wealth of the middle class.

Since all this wealth is at the top and rarely trickles down in any significant way, this creates economic and social oppression for people at the bottom. When people protest against this unjust situation, the cry against the protest is always the same: socialism. Yes, we have socialism, but it is for the rich one percent at the top that doesn't include most Americans. The spirit behind socialism is to make sure that the working class or the proletarian can meet their basic needs in a capitalistic society. It makes a case for the estate of the lowly in their effort to rebuild society to make it more just and humane. Reinhold Niebuhr states, "Who is better able to understand the true character of a civilization than those who suffer most from its limitations? Who is better able to state the social ideal in unqualified terms than those who have experienced the bankruptcy of old social realities in their lives?"[7] It is outright hypocritical to argue against socialism when it is among the very rich. There isn't anything wrong with sharing the resources in society with the mass of people who produce the resources. Even God shows cosmic socialism. "He makes His sun rise on the evil and on the good, and sends rain on the just and on the unjust (Matthew 5:45)." There is already a form of socialism existing within our capitalistic system. When there is a fire, firemen go to the location where the fire is regardless of class, zip code, race, and political persuasion. Just think if we could have a system that works this way in terms of the financial market. This form of socialism is not only with the fire department but also with the police department, paramedic service, Medicaid, Medicare, Social Security, etc. To protect the unjust economic system by decrying socialism, the real point of criticism should be directed at the oligarchs who make equalitarianism impossible within human society. Robert B. Reich wrote this about the oligarchs:

> As long as they control the purse strings, the oligarchs know there will be no substantial tax increase for them. Instead, their taxes will fall. There

---

7. Reinhold Niebuhr, *Moral Man and Immoral Society A Study in Ethics and Politics* (New York: Charles Scribner's Sons Publisher, 1932), 157.

will be no antitrust enforcement to puncture the power of their giant corporations. Instead, their corporations will grow larger. There will be no meaningful constraint on Wall Street's dangerous gambling addiction. There will be no limits to CEO pay, and Wall Street hedge fund and private equity managers will rake in billions of dollars more. Government will provide even more corporate subsidies, bailouts, and loan guarantees. It will continue to eliminate protections for consumers, workers, and the environment. It will become a government for, of, and by the oligarchy. The biggest political divide in America today is not between Republicans and Democrats. It's between democracy and oligarchy. Hearing and using the same old labels prevents most people from noticing they're being shafted.[8]

When the owners of production amass enormous wealth without giving their workers just wages to meet their basic needs, take care of their families, have health care, send their children to college, etc., this creates economic oppression brought on by unchecked capitalism. The argument is not against capitalism but its imbalance. Thus, we should look at democratic socialism to achieve democracy in the social and economic system. Again, the issue is not against the amassing of wealth but its fair distribution. "Wealth—to use a homely illustration—is to a nation what manure is to a farm. If the farmer spreads it evenly over the soil, it will enrich the whole. If he should leave it in heaps, the land will be impoverished and under the rich heaps, the vegetation would be killed."[9]

When owners of the market don't care about the working class but only about profit, we have a situation that can be described in the words of Victor Hugo, "There is always more misery among the lower classes than there is humanity in the higher."[10] If people were more humane and empathetic towards those who are down and out and need some help to get up, America and the world would be a better place to live. We could significantly wipe out hunger and homelessness if justice is done. But, since America and other nations are not as just as they could be, and since the

---

8. Robert B. Reich, *The System Who Rigged It, How We Fix It* (New York: Vintage Books A Division of Penguin Random House LLC, 2020), 17.
9. Walter Rauschenbusch, *Walter Rauschenbusch, Selected Writing*, edited by Winthrop S. Hudson (New York: Paulist Press, 1984), 146.
10. Victor Hugo, *Les Miserables*, 1862.

system that creates poverty goes unchallenged and untransformed, democracy is on the decline. As long as American Christianity is complicit by its abysmal silence, we are still afflicted with hunger, homelessness, and poverty in society. To snatch back American democracy, American Christianity must break its silence and join allegiance with other democracy fighters for the poor and working class to have a chance at life, liberty, and the pursuit of happiness. Walter Rauschenbusch, the social gospel scholar, made a very cogent observation:

> The failure of justice is evident in the system's allowing the rich to grow richer through unearned profit coming from such practices as speculative holding of land, control of extortionist monopolies, and ownership of natural resources and utilities vital to the community. Workers, on the other hand, receive for their hard-toil wages that are kept at the lowest level possible. Capitalism fails as badly when measured by the standard of liberty. Owners are ensnared in the dehumanizing grip of power and greed, while workers are captive to poverty and a system that allows them no control over their destiny. Finally, the system fails the test of brotherhood, for it gives owners autocratic power over workers and tempts workers to hatred of owners.[11]

Reinhold Niebuhr further states, "The blessings which Jesus pronounced upon the poor and the warnings he sounded against riches are justified by the recognition that there are temptations of riches which are too great to be overcome. They can only be escaped by voluntary or involuntary poverty. Special privileges make all men dishonest. The purest conscience and the clearest mind are prostituted by the desire to prove them morally justified."[12]

Jesus tells a parable about a man who went to hell because he refused to see his poor brother; he refused him justice and humanity. His name was Dives; he was a rich man with a surplus of resources. There was also a poor man by the name of Lazarus who had fallen on hard times, suffering from a deficient of resources. Not only was Lazarus poor and hungry, he was sick;

---

11. Walter Rauschenbusch, *Walter Rauschenbusch American Reformer* (New York: MacMillan Publishing Company, 1988), 170.
12. Reinhold Niebuhr, *Moral Man and Immoral Society*, 162.

sores were over his body from the crown of his head to the soles of his feet. Malnutrition had rendered him the inability to hardly move. But, somehow, he struggled to get to the gate of Dives, hoping to be fed the crumbs that fell from his table. The rich man was so selfish, disconnected, and heartless from feeling the infirmities of a brother in need that he did nothing to help poor Lazarus. The dogs had more compassion for Lazarus by licking his sores than the rich man ever showed. Dives refused to see the beggar at his gate. He was so caught up in his business affairs and social gatherings that the plight of Lazarus made no impression on him. Lazarus was invisible to Dives, just like the destitute people were across from the White House.

Dives was probably thinking like many people think today. "God help those who help themselves." This is partially true. Adam Hamilton said, "First, this phase is sometimes used as a way of avoiding our obligation as Christians to help others, of doing our part to love our neighbors. The fact is that some people truly cannot help themselves. And for many others who find themselves trapped in poverty or struggling financially, self-help often isn't nearly as simple as summoning the will and pulling themselves up by the bootstraps. Sometimes people are in a hole so deep that they can't climb out without help."[13] Unfortunately, Dives and many others today don't realize this.

But there comes a time when we all share something in common, and that is death. Death is the great equalizer. The story goes on to say that the poor and the rich man died, and they ended up in two different geographical locations. Lazarus landed in the bosom of Abraham, where there was peace and contentment, and Dives landed in Hell, where there was fire and anguish. A great gulf was fixed between the two. Dives could not get to Lazarus nor Lazarus to Dives, even though Dives made a desperate request for Lazarus to dip his finger in some water and cool his tongue. Abraham reminded Dives about his life of pleasure and ease and how the beggar at his gate made no impression on his soul; therefore, he could not matriculate into the Kingdom of Greatness. Let it be known that wealth didn't send Dives to hell. His class didn't send him to hell. His politics didn't send him to hell.

---

13. Adam Hamilton, *Half Truths God Helps Those Who Help Themselves And Other Things The Bible Doesn't Say* (Nashville: Abingdon Press, 2016), 61.

What sent Dives to hell is his cold-heartedness that he could not feel the suffering and needs of a fellow human being. He went to Hell because he was guilty of having what Frederick Douglass called "Too much religion and very little humanity."[14] He went to Hell because Martin Luther King, Jr said, "He maximized the minimum and minimized the maximum."[15] He went to Hell because he substituted what Martin Buber calls the "I-It relationship for the I-Thou relationship."[16] The I-It relationship is self-centered rather than other-centered. It sees people not as human beings but as objects to be exploited or ignored. This type of relationship leaves no room for human compassion and mercy. The I-Thou relationship is different. It reaches down to raise others. This relationship says, "I cannot be what I ought to be until you are what you ought to be."[17] John Donne understood this and said, "No man is an island entire of itself; every man is a piece of the continent, a part of the Maine."[18] Dives went to Hell because he failed to see this. Not only did Dives fail to see this, but America and other nations fail to see this, which carries eternal consequences. Therefore, we have choices that put us on a trajectory toward life with God or on a trajectory that takes us away from a life with God. Our choices are ours to make, and whatever choices we make, we cannot blame God for the outcome.

Some people may think that this parable does not apply to them because they are not rich in money. You don't have to be rich in money; you may be rich in other things that could aid others at the gate. Whatever we may have, great or small, there are beggars at the gate seeking physical and spiritual nourishment. Some are seeking the bread of hope, the bread of love, the bread of faith. They are asking for the crumbs that fall from our table, realizing that the crumbs have nourishment to lift up their beaten-down spirits. Howard Thurman said, "Little things can make a big difference. A little act of kindness at the moment of great need makes all the difference between sunshine and shadows. A smile at the right moment may make an intolerable burden lighter. Just a note bearing a message of

---

14. Frederick Douglass, *"Too Much Religion, Too Little Humanity,"* an address delivered in New York, New York, on May 9, 1849, in Blassingame, *The Frederick Douglass Papers*, 2:182-183.

15. Martin Luther King, Jr., *A Testament of Hope The Essential Writings of Martin Luther King, Jr.*, edited by James Melvin Washington (San Francisco: Harper & Row Publishers, 1986), 274.

16. Martin Buber, *I And Thou*, translated by Ronald Gregor Smith (T&T Clark, Publisher, February 1937).

17. Martin Luther King, Jr., *A Testament of Hope*, 269.

18. John Donne, *"For Whom The Bell Tolls,"* 1940.

simple interest or concern or affection may give to another the radically needed assurance."[19] There are beggars at our gate; Jesus told this parable to remind us as individuals and as a nation not to pass them by. We are our brothers' keepers, and Dives paid an eternal cost for not realizing this in time. We, too, will pay an eternal cost if we don't act now to right the wrongs of social and economic injustice. Those who have no concern or interest in justice will come under the Lord's condemnation.

When the tables turned, Dives woke up in hell, and Lazarus was comforted in heaven. Not only did Dives recognize his eternal location, but he also recognized the location of Lazarus. The man he paid no attention to, made no effort to give a helping hand, refused to recognize his humanity, turned a death ear to his plea for crumbs, denied him justice, and made invisible because of his cold heart, is now asking his host Abraham to allow Lazarus to come and dip the tip of his finger in water to cool is tongue because he is in torment in the fire. But Abraham said to him, "Son, remember that in your lifetime you received your good things, while Lazarus received bad things, but now he is comforted here, and you are in agony. And besides all this, between us and you, a great chasm has been set in place so that those who want to go from here to you cannot, nor can anyone cross over from there to us." The rich man suddenly becomes concerned about others when he showed no concern, at least to Lazarus. He wanted to go to his family to warn his five brothers to repent to avoid this place of torment. Maybe they will have a change of heart if someone from the dead rises and talks with them. But Abraham responded to him, "They have Moses and the Prophets; let them listen to them. If they do not listen to Moses and the Prophets, they will not be convinced even if someone rises from the dead (Luke 16:25-31)."

American Christians must understand that our otherworldly fate is set by our decisions on earth. If we fail to repent and become loving, just, and compassionate toward others, we too will be asking like the rich man for assistance that won't be granted. Therefore, it behooves us not to neglect to give justice and assistance to those in need when it is in our power to do so. Our neglect today means eternal regret tomorrow.

---

19. Howard Thurman, *The Mood of Christmas* (Richmond, IN: Friends United Press, 1985), 47.

Chapter Six

FRUITLESS CHRISTIANS

Just as a flower which seems beautiful and has color but no perfume, so are the fruitless words of the man who speaks them but does them not. —John Dewey

Producing fruit is an expectation of the Kingdom of God. Any tree that is supposed to produce fruit and doesn't is in danger of being cut down. When a tree has within it fruit-producing power and it fails to produce, something is terribly wrong with the tree. There could be a disease that is slowly killing the tree, which affects its producing fruit. If the disease is ignored, the tree may still stand and the leaves may cover the disease of the tree, nevertheless the tree is dying. This tree analogy is a representation of the Christian church that has been planted in the soil of the Kingdom of God to produce fruit. Evidently, there must be a disease in the tree because the Christian church is divided racially, denominationally, and theologically, causing the tree not to produce fruit for the Kingdom of God.

Many people come to the Christian church but are finding no fruit of love, justice, equality, and democracy. In fact, they are finding beautiful leaves but no fruit. They enter state-of-the-art buildings but often cannot find the spiritual and theological fruit that inspires actions to achieve justice in society. Often, what happens in the city, such as the unjustified killing of another black man by police, never gets spoken about in the worship service. There is a disconnect between what is really happening to people and what is going on in the Christian church, and we wonder why the Christian church is fruitless.

Statistics point out that unless the Christian church does serious reformation, there will only be empty shells of its former self. "We have been more concerned about building an institution than about building the church. The Protestant Reformation challenged and changed our understanding of salvation (soteriology), but it hardly touched our doctrine of church (ecclesiology). Because our ecclesiology was basically untouched by the Reformation, we are still trying to define church by 'building temples' or 'erecting tabernacles.'"[1] Jesus didn't come to earth to minister to brick and mortar, but to people, and if people are not our focus of ministry, then our ministry is meaningless. Jesus said, "The Spirit of the Lord is upon Me because He has anointed Me to preach the gospel to the poor; He has sent Me to heal the brokenhearted, to proclaim liberty to the captives and recovery of sight to the blind, to set at liberty those who are oppressed (Luke 4:18)." Loving, liberating, and lifting people from their downtrodden circumstances was the stock and trade of Jesus ministry on earth. He didn't start his ministry implying building physical structures. When Jesus told Peter, "Upon this rock, I will build my church (Matthew 16:18)," He was talking about building up His following on the solid rock of truth. When ideas, precepts, presuppositions, interpretations, principalities, and powers come to try to dismantle the Gospel of Christ, the truth shall still stand. Therefore, when building structures become more than building lives, we are participating in idolatry. This prompted Edward H. Hammett to say:

> The church has been more focused on those inside the walls than outside the walls. Members of the Christian community believe that the church was created for them, when in reality, the church is the only organization in society created for those outside it. When we turned inward and started caring only for each other, we lost sight of the poor and hurting of society (most of whom are not in an institutional church). Instead of keeping abreast of needs in our society, we spent our time, money, and energy

---

1. Edward H. Hammett, *Making the Church Work, Converting the Church for the 21st Century* (Macon, GA: Smyth & Helwys Publishing Inc., 2000), 87.

taking care of us! After doing this for so long, we found that we liked being taken care of by those we know and trust. We became insulated or isolated from those to whom Christ calls the church to minister.[2]

While on earth, Jesus showed us how to minister and to whom to minister. His ministry was not confined inside the church. In fact, the majority of Jesus's preaching, teaching, and miracles were outside the church. The parables He told were mostly on hill sides, mountain tops, and in the open plains. Jesus had a very skillful imagination and He used this imagination to tell parables to help us see ourselves in the spiritual mirror so we can make the necessary adjustments that would be pleasing to God. This is not to suggest that there were no other great teachers who told parables, but their teachings did not take on the quality of eternity, as did the teachings of Jesus to cover the whole spectrum of spirituality. We know what God is like; we know what God expects, and we know what God wants in return. The warnings and judgment of God are more fully understood because of the teaching and parables of Jesus.

In this parable of the barren fig tree, Jesus tells a story that "A man had a fig tree, planted in his vineyard, and he went to look for fruit on it but did not find any. So he said to the keeper of the vineyard, 'For three years now, I've been coming to look for fruit on this fig tree and haven't found any. Cut it down! Why should it use up the soil? 'Lord,' the keeper replied, 'leave it alone for one more year, and I'll dig around it and fertilize it. If it bears fruit next year, fine! If not, then cut it down."

Jesus tells this parable so we can see that the One who created the fig tree is God; the man who takes care of the vineyard is Jesus, and the fig tree is you and I. Whether we know it or not, God comes periodically and searches your life and mine and says, 'Still no fruit; still no humility; still no godliness; still no growth; still no maturity. God searches the Christian church and says, "Still no love; still no justice, still no equality, still no unity, 'Cut it down!' But Jesus says, 'Leave it alone for one more year, and I'll dig around it and fertilize it. If it bears fruit next year, fine! If not, then cut it down.'" The parable points out that God's judgment has begun and will be consummated in the near future, and if we are fruitless, our

---

2. Ibid., 87.

existence will be cut down. The Gardener of our lives knows that fruitless trees are detrimental to the soil. When fruitless trees don't produce, they take away the nutrients from fruitful trees that are producing.

Jesus Christ is digging around the socioeconomic tree of American society and fertilizing it with His grace and mercy. He has been pouring in His Word and Spirit so that we might bear fruit for the Kingdom of God, but to God's disappointment, American Christianity is still fruitless. There is still no justice, equality, and unity fruit found on the tree of society. American Christianity has been living in the soil of God's grace and mercy for over 400 years, but the only thing God has found on its tree is nothing but leaves. Leaves are the denial of freedom, justice, and equality. It is nothing but empty promises of which American creeds and deeds don't match. Martin Luther King, Jr. stated, "We talk eloquently about our commitment to the principles of Christianity, and yet our lives are saturated with the practice of paganism. We proclaim our devotion to democracy, but we sadly practice the very opposite of the democratic creed. We talk passionately about peace, and at the same time, we assiduously prepare for war. We make our fervent pleas for the high road of justice, and then we tread unflinchingly the low road of injustice."[3] American Christianity is still barren in love, fruitless in justice and sterile in racial integration. Eleven o'clock hour on Sunday morning is still the most segregated time in America. American Christianity is, by and large, still fruitless in justice and equality. It has become so fruitless it is in danger of being cut down. The socioeconomic political tree of society has produced nothing characteristically of the Kingdom of God. The social order is still racist; people are still homeless and hungry; the oppressed are still not liberated; the downtrodden are still not lifted up; the least of these are still overlooked, and the poor are still treated and defined by their poverty.

The God of Jesus Christ is searching the tree of American democracy and finding no fruit but leaves. Leaves of racism, leaves of white supremacy, leaves of greed, leaves of denied justice, leaves of empty promises, and leaves of theological and ecclesiastical hollowness. All of which is producing no fruit the Lord desires to find on a tree planted in the soil of His grace and

---

3. Martin Luther King, Jr., *Strength to Love* (Philadelphia: Fortress Press, 1963), 37.

mercy. This fruitlessness will continue because American Christianity sees no interconnectedness of religion, economic, social, and political linkage to create a just and moral society. As long as America continues to separate faith from politics justice from social and economic policies, the axe is laid at the root of the nation. Until America diagnoses and acknowledges the problem of its own sickness, it can never apply the right therapy. Joel Edward Goza stated, "Once we realize how inequality haunts our babies from the cradle to the classroom, from the classroom to the court room, from the employment application to the unemployment line, from sweat to equity, we see how the 'strange fruit' of broken black bodies represents only the tip of the iceberg of a system perfectly constructed to destroy black lives long before police lights ever flicker."[4]

For years America still has not produced the fruit of which God is searching for on the tree of its democracy. What else can God say other than "Cut it down?" Out of all the social movements that turned over the soil of America to get it to produce the fruit of justice, equality, and righteousness, and it is still fruitless, what else can God say but "Cut it down?" After the Emancipation Proclamation, Reconstruction, and the Civil Rights struggle, and systemic racism and sexism are still endemic in America's religious and socioeconomic institutions, what else can God say other than "Cut it down?" When "New forms of injustice for old ones and enthrone a new tyranny on the throne of the old,"[5] what else can God say to America but "Cut it down?" When the catholic and evangelical churches remain reticent about racial injustice and police killings of unarmed black people, what else can God say other than "Cut it down?" When a tree produces no fruit for the Kingdom of God while sapping up the nutrients of the soil, what else can God say other than "Cut it down?"

When religion is only concerned about the souls of people as Martin Luther King Jr. said, "And is not equally concerned about the slums that damn them, the economic conditions that strangle them, and the social conditions that cripple them," what else can God say other than "Cut it down?" God is not interested in leaves on trees but its fruit. When a nation like America has been blessed with so much, and there is still no fruit of

---

4. Joel Edward Goza, *America's UnHoly Ghosts, The Racist Roots of Our Faith and Politics* (Eugene, OR: Cascade Books, imprint of Wipf & Stock Publishers, 2019), 24.

5. Reinhold Niebuhr, *Moral Man And Immoral Society,* 262.

justice, equality, and dignity, God is saying, "Cut it down." When Christians only have leaves of ecclesiastical rites and ceremonies but no fruit, God is saying, "Cut it down! Why should it use up the soil?"

How much longer America has to produce the fruit God is searching for is unknown. But, what is known is nations that didn't produce the fruit of justice, peace, equality, and morality no longer exist. Our Gardner, Jesus Christ, is saying, "Lord, leave it alone for another year. Let me tend it a little more. Let me water it a little more. Let me pull out the weeds of racism, injustice, inequality, and immorality and dig around it. Allow Me to pour living water in the soil and fertilize it with the living Word to see if the American tree of democracy will produce. If not, cut it down!" These words of Jesus are America's warning that time is of the essence. The nation is given another chance, another opportunity, filled with amazing potential to bear fruit for the Kingdom of God. It doesn't matter how old or young we may be; there is still an opportunity to bear fruit. Again, God is not interested in the leaves of our trees but its fruit. God is not interested in how tall or short our trees are. God is not interested in how narrow or how wide our trees are. God is interested in the fruit of our trees. Every fruit-bearing tree that doesn't bear fruit is in danger of being cut down. Jesus said, "I am the true vine, and my Father is the gardener. He cuts off every branch in me that bears no fruit, while every branch that does bear fruit he prunes so that it will be even more fruitful (John 15:1-2)."

Fruit bearing is what God is interested in, and if we cannot show God anything but leaves, we stand in danger of being cut down. Looking good and attractive on the outside does not impress God. Eloquent speaking and lip service alone cannot produce fruit. Religion without substance, faith without work, and Christian profession without Christian practice stand in danger of being cut down. God created life to produce. Seeds are within fruits to produce more fruit. God's Word is a seed that has been planet in the tree of every believer so the believer can bring forth more believers, so justice can produce more justice, so equality can produce more equality, and morality can produce more morality. But, when we fail to produce, and we are in good soil, God says, "Cut it down." When I look at America as Isaiah looked at Israel, I hope not to lament these same words:

DEPART FROM ME

      I will sing for the one I love
        a song about his vineyard:
      My loved one had a vineyard
        on a fertile hillside.
      He dug it up and cleared it of stones
        and planted it with the choicest vines.
      He built a watchtower in it
        and cut out a winepress as well.
      Then he looked for a crop of good grapes,
        but it yielded only bad fruit.

    "Now you dwellers in Jerusalem and people of Judah
      judge between me and my vineyard.
    What more could have been done for my vineyard
      than I have done for it?
    When I looked for good grapes,
      why did it yield only bad?
      Now I will tell you
    what I am going to do to my vineyard:
      I will take away its hedge,
        and it will be destroyed;
      I will break down its wall,
        and it will be trampled.
      I will make it a wasteland,
        neither pruned nor cultivated,
      and briers and thorns will grow there.
      I will command the clouds
        not to rain on it."
      The vineyard of the Lord Almighty
        is the nation of Israel,
      and the people of Judah
        are the vines he delighted in.
      And he looked for justice, but saw bloodshed;
    for righteousness, but heard cries of distress. Isaiah 5:1-7

God is saying to American Christianity, bear fruit or be cut off; bear fruit or your tree shall be cut down. The Holy Inspector is coming, and God is pointing out that leaves won't suffice. Your worship won't suffice; your seminars and conferences won't suffice. No fruit, no continued existence in Christ. Fruitless Christians will be cut off and destroyed. "Fruitless branches represent counterfeit disciples—people who were never really saved. They do not abide in Christ, the True Vine; they are not truly United with Him by faith. They are Judas branches. They can bear no genuine fruit. In the end, the Father removes them to preserve the life and fruitfulness of the other branches . . . Barren branches have nothing to look forward to except awful, fiery judgment. Yet the corresponding truth is equally blessed . . . As He carefully prunes and tends to us, there may be some pain in the cutting. But we can be certain that He is doing it for our own good so that we will bear fruit for His glory."[6]

---

6. John MacArthur, *The Gospel According to Jesus What Is Authentic Faith?* (Zondervan, 1988), 172.

Chapter Seven
TRAVELING THE WRONG ROAD

> *If someone is going down the wrong road, he doesn't need motivation to speed him up. What he needs is education to turn him around.* —Jim Rohn

Often time in life, people and nations can lose their way. They often become victims of their own doing. They travel down a road that looks like it's the right way for success and prosperity but later discover the road is the wrong way. Unless they get off the road they are traveling, it could lead to their destruction. Too many people and nations in human history have been destroyed following leaders, friends, and influences. People get caught up in the euphoria of the crowd, the charisma of leaders, and the peer pressure of friends, that cause them to go down a road that leads to their deep regret. Many things lead people down the wrong road. One that stands out among many is misinformation. When people have been misinformed, this leads to misjudgment, which leads to misdeeds.

To avoid being led down a dark and deadly road, there must be intentionality on the part of people to get all the facts and then make a wise decision about which road to travel. Facts are like pieces of a puzzle. We have to put the puzzle together to see the whole picture. Until all the pieces are put together, it is unwise to make rash decisions. Unfortunately, people make decisions before they see the whole picture. In doing so, they destroy allies they believe are enemies; they destroy friends they view as enemies and destroy opportunities they think are obstacles. A lot of decisions are made without seeing the whole picture, and once we travel down the road of our decision, we may have to travel for a while before we can get off. A lot can happen while traveling this road. We could have a breakdown in the common good, a breakdown in health, in the family, in the community, and in the nation. When people and nations choose the road of racism, oppression, injustice, and inhumanity, they are headed toward destruction. There can be no peace on the road of injustice, no safety on the road of greed, and no brotherhood on the road of oppression. It behooves every nation to make wise decisions before deciding to travel a particular road.

America is ranked number 27 in the world in education and healthcare. When people are denied access to opportunities, the nation can be no stronger than is weakest link. Historically, look at how people of color have been denied participating in democracy, and we wonder why America is ranked 27 among other nations. The racial strife in the nation has created fear, and when a nation fears itself, it cannot win on a global scale. Past and present racism has destroyed and is yet destroying America's ranking in the world. When America fails to invest in the best of minds because of the color of people's skin, America will continue to be left behind in other nations. When America refuses to invest in good healthcare for its citizens, the nation won't be healthy compared to other nations. When America refuses to invest in education for its citizens, how can the nation compete in the global market? Traveling the road of racism, injustice, inequality, and greed makes the nation weaker, not stronger. When people feel left out, overlooked, and denied participating in democracy, how can this build morale and make the nation safe? Frederick Douglass said, "Where justice is denied, where poverty is enforced, where ignorance prevails, and where any one class is made to feel that society is an organized conspiracy to oppress, rob and degrade them, neither persons nor property will be safe."[1] How can people feel patriotic when they have been treated unjustly? America is

---

1. Frederick Douglass, Speech on the 24th Anniversary of the Emancipation Proclamation, 1886, Washington D.C.

on a great decline, and unless America gets off this road she is traveling, the fear of becoming a second or third-rate nation will come true.

A growing sense of unease presently pervades the American consciousness. Americans are no longer as confident in their nation and self-assured as they once were. A sense of frustration and anger underscores American consciousness. Americans are looking over their shoulder at other emerging economic juggernauts and wondering if we can still be the world's social, political, and economic leader when Congress cannot even manage to balance the national budget. The thought that we are diminishing in stature in the eyes of the international community constantly torments Americans. Faded glory strikes a crippling blow to the American psyche. Analogous to an aging beauty queen, America might still possess a golden crown, but she lost her luster. In an eroding empire, Americans feel like second-class citizens in the union of nations.[2]

The great ongoing decline of America is self-inflicted. It is not that there weren't warning signs on the road the nation was traveling. Arrogance and outright rebellion against justice and equality are the main culprits for the nation's decline. When justice is denied, God is denied, and when God is denied, the nation becomes a reproach. Like ancient Israel, who wouldn't listen and repent and had to suffer the consequences of the nation's rebellion, America could suffer similarly. Jeremiah pointed out to Israel:

> And though the Lord has sent all his servants, the prophets, to you again and again, you have not listened or paid any attention. They said, "Turn now, each of you, from your evil ways and your evil practices, and you can stay in the land the Lord gave to you and your ancestors for ever and ever. Do not follow other gods to serve and worship them; do not arouse my anger with what your hands have made. Then I will not harm you." But you did not listen to me," declares the Lord, "and you have aroused my anger with what your hands have made, and you have brought harm to yourselves." Therefore, the Lord Almighty says this: "Because you have not listened to my words, I will summon all the peoples of the north and my servant Nebuchadnezzar, king of Babylon," declares the Lord, "and I will bring them against this land and its inhabitants and against all the

---

2. Kilroy J. Oldster, *Dead Toad Scrolls*, published by booklocker.com, 2016; cited from goodreads.com.

surrounding nations. I will completely destroy them and make them an object of horror and scorn and an everlasting ruin. I will banish from them the sounds of joy and gladness, the voices of bride and bridegroom, the sound of millstones and the light of the lamp. This whole country will become a desolate wasteland, and these nations will serve the king of Babylon for seventy years (Jeremiah 25:4-11).

Like Jeremiah, there were voices in America trying to get the nation to travel a different road because the present road of slavery, racism, inequality, and greed only leads to decline and destruction. Theodore Weld made this appeal to America:

> The slaveholders of the present generation, if cloven down by God's judgment, cannot plead that they were unwarned . . . Well, may the God of the oppressed cry out against them, "because I have called and ye have refused . . . Therefore will I laugh at your calamity and mock when your fear cometh. When your fear cometh like desolation and destruction and destruction like a whirlwind, then shall ye call, but I will not answer.[3]

David Walker made an appeal to America about sin and retribution of the justice of God. He attacked white preachers of American Christianity for supporting slavery and oppression.

> They have newspapers and monthly periodicals, which they receive in continual succession, but on the pages of which, you will scarcely ever find a paragraph respecting slavery, which is ten thousand times more injurious to this country than all the other evils put together, and which will be the final overthrow of its government, unless something is very speedily done; for their cup is nearly full.—Perhaps they will laugh at or make light of this; but I tell you Americans! that unless you speedily alter your course, you and your Country are gone! For God, Almighty will tear up the very face of the earth.[4]

---

3. Theodore Weld to Angelina, Feb. 6, 1842, from Gayraud S. Wilmore, *Black Religion And Black Radicalism* (Maryknoll, NY: Orbis Books, 1989), 29.
4. Ibid., 41.

America created Nat Turner because the nation would not travel the road of justice, equality, and humanity. Out of the crucible of slavery, Nat Turner saw himself as God's judgment on slave holders. Turner said:

> ... and on the appearance of the sign [the eclipse of the sun in February 1831], I should arise and prepare myself and slay my enemies with their own weapons. And immediately on the sign appearing in the heavens, the seal was removed from my lips, and I communicated the great work laid out for me to do to four in whom I had the greatest confidence [Henry Porter, Hark Travis, Nelson Williams, and Sam Francis are referred to here]. It was intended by us to have begun the work of death on the 4th of July last.[5]

Ironically, Frederick Douglass, on the 4th of July, also warned America in a speech given on Independence Day.

> Americans! Your republican politics, not less than your religion, are flagrantly inconsistent. You boast of your love of liberty, your superior civilization, and your pure Christianity, while the whole political power of the nation is solemnly pledge to support and perpetuate the enslavement of three million of your countrymen ... The existence of slavery in this country brands your republicanism as a sham, your humanity as a base pretense, and your Christianity as a lie ... Oh, Be warned! Be warned! A horrible reptile is coiled up in your nation's bosom; the venomous creature is nursing at the tender breast of your youthful republic; for the love of God, tear away and fling from you the hideous monster, and let the weight of twenty million crush and destroy it forever![6]

In 1902, Francis J. Grimke continued the warning to America in the early 20th Century. He spoke with power and said:

> God is not dead—nor is he an indifferent onlooker at what is going on in this world. One day, He will make restitution for blood; He will call the

---

5. Ibid., 68
6. Frederick Douglass, "The Meaning of July 4th for the Negro," Foner, ed., *Life and Writings*, 2:199, 201.

oppressors to account. Justice may sleep, but it never dies. The individual, race, or nation which does wrong, which sets at defiance God's great law, especially God's great law of love, of brotherhood, will be sure, sooner or later, to pay the penalty. We reap as we sow. With that measure we mete, it shall be measured to us again.[7]

Howard Thurman, the great mystic theologian who influenced a lot of Civil Rights leaders and who led a multiethnic congregation, said:

> Unless there is a great rebirth of high and holy moral courage, which will place at the center of our vast power an abiding sense of moral responsibility, both because of our treatment of minorities at home and our arrogance abroad, we may very easily become the most hated nation on earth. No amount of power, wealth, or prestige can stay this judgment. If we would be beloved, we must share that kind of spirit as the expression of the true genius of our democratic government.[8]

Martin Luther King, Jr. further warned, "A nation that continues year after year to spend more money on military defense than on programs of social uplift is approaching spiritual death."[9] From Nat Turner to Frederick Douglass to John Brown to Howard Thurman to Martin Luther King, Jr and others, America has been duly warned of its slavery, racism, and militarism. To this day, America has not heeded the warning nor corrected the structural problems of poverty, racism, and injustice. Unless America turns from the unjust practices against the poor, the oppressed, and the marginalized, the nation will continue to decline. We are already in moral and spiritual decline, and how much more or less the decline the nation undergoes depends on the nation's willingness to get off the road of injustice and inequality.

C. S. Lewis said, "We all want progress. But progress means getting nearer to the place where you want to be. And if you have taken a wrong turning, then to go forward does not get you any nearer. If you are on the wrong road, progress means doing an about-turn and walking back to the

---

7. Carter G. Woodson, Editor, *The Works of Francis J. Grimke* (Washington, DC: Associated Publishers, 1942), vol. 1, 354.

8. Howard Thurman, *Deep River and the Negro Spiritual Speaks of Life and Death* (Richmond, IN: Friends United Press, 1975), 59.

9. Martin Luther King, Jr. "Beyond Vietnam" Speech at the Riverside, April 4, 1967.

right road and in that case, the [nation] who turns back soonest is the most progressive man. There is nothing progressive about being pig-headed and refusing to admit a mistake. And I think if you look at the present state of the world it's pretty plain that humanity has been making some big mistake. We're on the wrong road. And if that is so, we must go back. Going back is the quickest way on."[10]

America's future depends on what decisions the nation makes today. No person or nation has to continue traveling on the wrong road. There are signs that can guide us off the road to destruction. The question is will the travelers notice and obey the signs before it is too late?

Jesus entered human history to get humanity off the road that leads to death, hell, and destruction. People and nations were traveling the natural road of war, conquest, oppression, power, and privilege. This road produced in humankind arrogance, hedonism, vanity, bitterness, and destruction. This cycle would repeat itself over and over again in human history. God sent His law and the prophets but humans failed to travel the high road of peace, justice, equality, and brotherhood. Then God sent His only begotten Son, who is "The way, the truth and the life (John 14:6)." Jesus is God's embodiment compass that leads us into the Kingdom of God, and if we follow Jesus the compass, not only will humankind be on the right road, but will get to our eternal destination. There were many roads people traveled trying to get to eternal existence. There was the compass of Hinduism, Buddhism, Confucianism, Taoism, Jainism, Sikhism, Zoroastrianism, Judaism, Islam, and many more compasses mankind used on the road to get from earth to heaven. Jesus simplified the direction. Since He came from heaven, He knows how to lead us into the Kingdom of God. Since Jesus is the Logos, the Word of God made flesh; He knows how to get us from earth to heaven. He knows how to get us from earth to heaven. Jesus is the great Navigator; He is heaven's GPS and the voice that directs us on the road when we need to make a turn or have made a wrong turn. The voice of the Holy Spirit is God through Christ, guiding us on the road of life. If we listen, we will get to our destination.

Unfortunately, many Christians are on the wrong road. Many churches are on the wrong road. People from every race, creed, and color are on

---

10. C. S. Lewis, *Mere Christianity* (HarperOne, 2015), 28–29.

the wrong road if their love for anything is more than doing justice, loving mercy, and walking humbly with God. Sadly, America seems to be choosing power over people, money over morality, position over principle, and entitlement over equality. The road that could get America to a more perfect union where we can have life, liberty, and the pursuit of happiness is being less traveled than the broad wrong road that leads to death, hell, and destruction. Out of all the social movements to encourage America to travel the road of its own creeds, America is choosing the opposite. Benjamin Mays said, "We used to believe, like Socrates, that evil and wrongdoing were based upon ignorance; that men fought wars because they didn't know any better; that racial prejudice was based on a lack of knowledge; that man exploited man because he needed to be enlightened. But we know now that knowledge is not enough; that man can know the truth and deliberately lie, see the good and deliberately choose evil, see the light and deliberately walk in darkness, see the 'high road' beckoning to [them] and deliberately choose the 'low road.'"[11] America cannot be all she espouses as long as the nation continues to travel on the wrong road. Regardless of the many exit signs that read: repent, must be born again, seek first the Kingdom of God, cannot serve two masters, confess with your mouth and believe in your heart, and walk in the Spirit, the nation continues to ignore, and American Christianity continues to aid and abet on the road to destruction. It doesn't take a rocket scientist to know that America and its Christianity cannot travel two roads at the same time, and Jesus makes it plain that there are only two roads in life to travel. We must choose one or the other.

The first road Jesus described is the broad road. Crowds of people are traveling this road. There are so many people on this broad road you cannot number them because they are increasing by the minute! Some are overtly, and others are covertly traveling this road. There are camouflaged Christians on this broad road: Republicans, Democrats, independents, conservatives, liberals, rich, poor, educated, uneducated, husbands, wives, children, and people of every description are on this broad road. The broad road is attractive; it is alluring; it is exciting; it is the feel-good road, the freedom of expression road. People can live like they want, do as they want, as long

---

11. Benjamin Mays, *Quotable Quotes of Benjamin Mays* (New York: Vantage Press, 1983), 10.

as they want. It is the road where people "Establish their own righteousness but will not submit to the righteous of God (Romans 10:3)." It is the road of cheap grace. "Grace [people] bestow on [themselves] . . . the preaching of forgiveness without requiring repentance, baptism without church discipline, Communion without confession . . . grace without discipleship, grace without the cross, grace without Jesus Christ, living and incarnate."[12]

It is the ear-tickling road where people are hearing what they want to hear. This is the road where people just want entertainment, not moral ethics. On this road, nothing is absolutely right, and nothing is absolutely wrong. It is the road of whatever the majority is doing it must be right. It is the road where principles and values don't matter. As long as you get what you want, the end justifies the means. It is the road of excuses, excuses for unrighteousness and un-commitment; It is the road of elitism, where money, position, and title are more important than the soul. It is the road of racism, narcissism, materialism, and militarism; the road where popularity is more important than being prophetic, politics is more important than prayer meetings, and civil pursuits are more important than spiritual gains. It is the road of "Manipulation, like the conquest whose objectives it serves, attempts to anesthetize the people so they will not think."[13] This is the road where you comfortably travel without standing up for anything but going along with everything. It is the road where immorality is reaching new lows; nightclubs are growing by leaps and bounds. It is the road where the bright lights, the night lights, the disco lights, and the blinking lights keep you excited and entertained to encourage you to stay on this road. There are some exit signs on this road, such as Substance Abuse Street. Do Your Thing Avenue. Casino Boulevard. Sex in the City Lane. There are also rest stops called Apathy Bypass and Complacency Drive. These are some but not all of the descriptions of the broad road that leads to death, hell, and destruction. Throngs of people are traveling on this road, and many don't realize where it is leading them.

Then Jesus describes another road, which he calls the strait gate or the narrow road. Very few people travel this road. This road is narrow and constrained. You cannot live like you want and say what you want on this

---

12. Dietrich Bonhoeffer, *The Cost of Discipleship*, trans. R. H. Fuller and Irmgard Booth, revised (New York: Macmillan, 1959), 35–36.

13. Paulo Freire, *Pedagogy of the Oppressed*, translated by Myra Bergman Ramous (New York: Continuum Publishing Company, 1999), 130.

road. You cannot fulfill the lust of the flesh on this road. You cannot serve two masters on this road. You cannot eat at the Lord's table of grace and mercy and the devil's table of racism and white supremacy. You cannot be double-minded and double-tongued on this road. On this road, you cannot be camouflaged as a builder when you are a destroyer. This is a road of justice, love, peace, and brotherhood. Its travelers are disciples committed to advancing the Kingdom of God in the midst of suffering and opposition. On this, God travelers hate what God hates and loves what God loves. This road doesn't have all the dazzling allurements and exciting lights that are on the board road. To travel this road is to receive a lot of criticism, opposition, persecution, and misunderstanding. On this road, not many people support you, and you have to bear a cross along the way. This road requires obedience and self-denial. It requires you to "Love your enemies; bless them that curse you, do good to them that hate you, and pray for them which despitefully use and persecute you (Matthew 5:44)." On this road, you respect and honor your parents, and parents respect and honor their children. It requires "Love is without dissimulation. You abhor evil and cleave to good. You are kindly affectioned one to another with brotherly love . . . Not slothful in business; fervent in spirit; serving the Lord; rejoicing in hope; patient in tribulation; and continuing in prayer (Romans 12:9-12)." Because of the principles, ethics, and spiritual requirements on this strait and narrow road, there are not many travelers.

Every now and then, you come across a traveler—who is committed to discipleship, praying for the weak, praising God for social and economic progress, standing up against injustice, resisting the tentacles of evil, and totally involved with the work of the Kingdom of God. There are hills and mountains, steep curves, rough overpasses, and dangerous embankments. The winds of adversity blow on this road. Storms and violent winds of misunderstanding blow on this road. There are exit signs that read: Don't get weary in Well Doing Boulevard; Trust in the Lord Lane; I Am With You Always Drive; Restoration Circle; Refuge and Strength Crossing; Peace Unto You Square. There are rest stops as well called Revival Place, Prayer Meeting and Bible Study Alley, and Press On Bypass. Jesus reminds travelers the strait and narrow road is the path that leads from the kingdom of this world to the Kingdom of God.

American Christianity must choose which road to travel. The United States and the postmodern church are standing at the crossroads of life. Our government, our society, our financial institutions, our schools, and the postmodern church are divided, and the future of our nation and generations hang in the balance. We cannot delay which road to travel and we cannot travel two roads at the same time. We must choose now, or the forces of darkness will choose for us. If we continue to stand on the sideline watching the moral decline of our nation, we also shall watch its great downfall. God told the nation of Israel, "I call heaven and earth as witnesses today against you, that I have set before you life and death, blessing ad cursing; therefore choose life, that you and your descendants may live (Deuteronomy 30:19)." God too is encouraging America to choose the right road. James Russel Lowell said, "Once to every man and nation comes a moment to decide, in the strife of truth and falsehood, for the good or evil side; some great cause, God's new Messiah offering each the gloom or blight, and the choice goes by forever 'twixt that darkness and that light."[14] We either choose the road of justice, equality, and dignity or continue to travel the road of least resistance, where racism, inequality, and white supremacy will surely lead to the death of this republic. A crossroad decision can be tough because we know if we make the wrong decision, it can have life long consequences. Robert Frost captures the tough position we are in at the crossroads:

> Two roads diverged in a yellow wood,
> And sorry I could not travel both
> And be one traveler, long I stood
> And looked down one as far as I could
> To where it bent in the undergrowth.
> I shall be telling this with a sigh
> Somewhere ages and ages hence:
> Two roads diverged in a wood, and
> I took the one less traveled by,
> And that has made all the difference.[15]

---

14. James Russell Lowell, "*The Present Crisis*," December 1845.
15. Robert Frost, "The Road Not Taken," *A Selection of Robert Frost's Poems* (New York: H. Holt and Co, 1991).

To decide which road to take at the crossroads must be thought out carefully and prayerfully because the direction we choose will have ramifications for the rest of our lives and the future of the nation. We all want to get to the destination of life, liberty, and the pursuit of happiness. However, history reveals that no nation can sustain itself when there is an enormous gap between the rich and poor, the have and the have-nots. The unraveling of the nation begins to show signs when discontentment of the marginalized fills the air and people feel they have nothing to lose in their pursuit to gain for themselves what others refuse to grant. Those who withhold socioeconomic justice from the poor and oppressed are actually providing the fuel for revolutionary activity. Here is where American Christianity is either authentic or a farce. If American Christianity sides with oppressors as it has in the past and present, then it is a farce. It is a farce not because it stands for "law and order" but become it refuses to take under consideration ordered injustice that creates the conditions that cause the discontentment of the oppressed in the first place.

When revolutionary activity begins, it is transgressing the boundary set by the oppressor, of which violence is released on the oppressed to maintain the oppressive situation. To claim "law and order" without assessing the justice of the law or its equitable distribution is to look through the lens of the oppressor to justify his violence against the oppressed. "Whereas the violence of the oppressors prevents the oppressed from being fully human, the response of the latter to this violence is grounded in the desire to pursue the right to be human. As the oppressors dehumanize others and violate their rights, they also become dehumanized. As the oppressed, fighting to be human (and have justice), take away the oppressors' power to dominate and suppress, they restore to the oppressors the humanity they had lost in the exercise of oppression."[16] To avoid a costly and bloody revolution, it behooves oppressors to give up their oppression and American Christianity to give up its complicity with it and practice justice and fairness toward the poor and oppressed. The absence of justice is the presence of tension, which leads to no peace. Who knows, when the water dam of resistance burst forth, there might be no time to defuse and control the situation. The time is now to give up those things that divide and separate us from having

---

16. Paulo Freire, *Pedagogy of the Oppressed*, translated by Myra Bergman Ramos, 38.

full democracy in the nation. We cannot keep saying, "God bless America" when Isaiah reminds us, "Your iniquities have separated you from God, and your sins have hidden His face from you so that He will not hear (Isaiah 59:2)." It is a dangerous situation to be in when God—the Creator of the universe—separates and hides from the nation that refuses to repent. It is worse than a threatening nuclear bomb. A decision must be made.

In making our decision as a nation, Martin Luther King, Jr. left us these words:

> "The choice is ours, and though we might prefer it otherwise, we must choose in this crucial moment of human history. And if we will only make the right choice, we will be able to transform this pending cosmic elegy into a creative psalm of peace. If we will make the right choice, we will be able to transform the jangling discords of our world into a beautiful symphony of brotherhood. If we will but make the right choice, we will be able to speed up the day, all over America and all over the world, when 'Justice will roll down like waters, and righteousness like a mighty stream.'"[17]

The choice and consequences are ours!

---

17. Martin Luther King, Jr. *"Beyond Vietnam—A Time to Break Silence"* April 4, 1967, Riverside Church, New York City.

Chapter Eight
LUKEWARM CHRISTIANS

Lukewarm people don't really want to be saved from their sin; they want only to be saved from the penalty of their sin.
—Francis Chan

We receive news on a daily basis, and the weather report is part of our daily news. We often tune in to the weather report so we can plan our day accordingly. We want to know about the temperature and the forecast to see what kind of weather we should expect for today and the rest of the week. The weather report helps us to determine what clothes to wear, light or heavy, so we are prepared for what the day holds. The weather report is a forecast so we are not caught off guard in light of a storm that may be looming near. We have grown accustomed to the weather and temperature reports in the daily news. Also, we are accustomed to a temperature check when we visit the doctor. Before the doctor sees us, a temperature report is taken so the doctor is aware of our present vital signs. Temperature is extremely important. It is important for our existence; it is important for the food we eat. If food doesn't keep the right temperature, it spoils and is unfit to eat. Temperature is important for the homes we live in and the places we work. Having the right temperature is central to the functionality of our daily lives.

When was the last time we heard about the temperature of the church, and why must Christians pay attention to its temperature? The temperature of the church ought to motivate us to prepare for what is looming ahead. Our current times point to the return of Jesus Christ at any time. Is the Christian church prepared to meet the Great Physician? Does the church have the right temperature in light of the current toxicity of our land? We can clearly see how the precipitation of sin is coming down so heavy that "We are calling immorality, morality, light darkness and darkness light; we are calling good evil and evil good. We are calling sweet bitter and bitter sweet (Isaiah 5:20)." What used to be shameful and taboo is now lifted up as heroic and courageous. The moral temperature of America doesn't look good. Racial hostility, injustice, insurrection, and government division have raised the nation's temperature to a high fever level, and our nation is feeling sick with the chills of white supremacy. Unless we lower the temperature by listening and dialoguing with one another, America will die an untimely death. The high fever of racism, cynicism, fascism, and political defeatism must be given a dose of acetaminophen so America's defense mechanism can fight the infection in the body politic. Racism is the greatest existential threat to the wellness of the nation, and until we treat racism as a threat and not as a triumph of white supremacy, the fever it produces will cause the body of the nation to succumb to its infectious disease. America cannot maintain this high temperature of racism and injustice because the high fever will damage the body of the nation, and its organs will start shutting down. Treating the symptoms and not the cause of the infection in the body will only delay the inevitable.

Given how we prepare for snowstorms, sleet and ice, hurricanes, thunderstorms, and earthquakes, we need to prepare to do surgery on America before it is too late. We also need to prepare for the greatest forthcoming event in human history, and that is the coming of Jesus Christ, our Lord! Jesus reminds us that:

> "As it was in the days of Noah, so will it be at the coming of the Son of Man. For in the days before the flood, people were eating and drinking, marrying and giving in marriage, up to the day that Noah entered the ark. They were oblivious until the flood came and swept them all away. So will it be at the coming of the Son of Man. Two men will be in the field: one will be taken and the other left. Two women will be grinding at the mill:

one will be taken and the other left. Therefore keep watch, because you do not know the day on which your Lord will come (Matthew 24:37-42)."

Just as we should watch for the coming of Jesus Christ we must also watch the temperature of our nation, and especially the temperature of the church because it is the Body of Christ. Jesus wants Christians to pay attention to the temperature of the church because if the church's vital organs start shutting down, then the same happens to the community, society, and the nation. The temperature of the church must be just right to function as it should to advance the Kingdom of God on earth. When an infection like racism and injustice gets into the body of the church, it weakens the church, and the church loses its power and effectiveness in the world.

I mention infection because the virus of racism and injustice has been in the body of the church since the colonial period and has created an infection that needs heavy doses of antibiotics. What are the prescribed antibiotics for the church? It is the Word and Spirit of God that convicts, washes and heals. "If my people who are called by My name will humble themselves, and pray and seek My face, and turn from their wicked ways, then I will hear from heaven and will forgive their sin and heal their land (2 Chronicles 7:14)." There can be no healing without repentance; no reconciliation without justice, and the American church is in need of both.

Jesus Christ does not want the church to perish along with the world. He knows the American church does not have the right temperature. Therefore, He has sent spiritual meteorologists, such as pastors and prophets, to give the present temperature of the church. If the pastors refuse to be prophets and tell the truth about the present temperature of the church, then these pastors are rotten religionists who are hirelings, not shepherds. Congregations will do well to assess and evaluate what kind of pastor is leading them. Pastors are supposed to know the temperature of the church, and when the church is lukewarm concerning wrong, evil, injustice and inequality, and those things that stifle the Kingdom of God, pastors are supposed to tell the truth even thou it may cost them their pulpits. Instead of helping the church to have the right temperature, many pastors and theologians of the past and present "Provided a moral rationale for slavery, succession, and the development of Southern nationalism."[1]

---

1. Kenneth Cauthen, *I Don't Care What the Bible Says* (Macon GA: Mercer University Press, 2003), 50.

Pastors, white and black, brown and yellow, have a choice: either encourage the church to be hot or cold because lukewarmness is unacceptable to the King of Kings and Lord of Lords. Neutrality supports what is rather than what ought to be. It is the guarantor of the status quo. Elie Wiesel said,

> "We must take sides. Neutrality helps the oppressor, never the victim. Silence encourages the torment, never the tormented. Sometimes, we must interfere. When human lives are endangered, when human dignity is in jeopardy, national borders and sensitivities become irrelevant. Whenever men and women are persecuted because of their race, religion, or political views, that place must—at that moment—become the center of the universe."[2]

How often has the church been silent about the suffering and oppression of African Americans in this country? How often have their suffering been shoved to the periphery of American society and not made the center of our nation's concern enough to wipeout systematic racism? American Christianity must choose before it is too late.

Jesus speaks to the church of the Laodiceans because they did not know the profound trouble they were in. They did not know they didn't have the right temperature, and it spoiled the Bread of Life in their midst. The Laodiceans thought they were doing just fine. They had money in the bank; they were living comfortable lives; they saw themselves as a success story. They had all of the outer appearances of material success, but they were unaware of their spiritual temperature. They gave half-baked sermons, half-baked prayers, half-baked revivals, half-baked evangelism, and half-baked praise—if they praised at all. They thought they were doing fine. They were in lock step with the status quo while overtly staying out of social, economic, and political issues but covertly supporting them. They refused to involve themselves in comforting the afflicted and afflicting the comfortable. They chose not to suffer for justice and righteousness because the cultural norms were more important than the crucified Christ. They had no sense of urgency to get involved with the struggle against structural

---

2. Elie Wiesel, Nobel Peace Prize acceptance speech on Dec. 10, 1986.

injustice, poverty, housing issues, police brutality, exploitation of the poor, and the lack of access to the marginalized. They practiced quietism. William R. Jones described quietism this way:

> Quietism . . . is a refusal to reform the status quo, especially where traditional institutions and values are involved. Conformity, accommodation and acquiescence are its distinguishing marks. Quietism becomes our operating principle if we believe that esp (economic, social, and political) correction is unnecessary, impossible, or inappropriate. Corrective action is unnecessary, for instance, if we believe that some agent other than ourselves will handle it. Another quietist tendency is found in the familiar adage, 'If it ain't broke, don't fix it.' . . . We are also pushed to quietism if remedial action is thought to be impossible. We reach this conclusion, it appears, when we encounter an invincible force or when the item to be corrected is a structure of ultimate reality. Finally, change is rejected if changing things will make it worse.[3]

The Laodiceans were in their religious bubble, doing church without being the church. Their focus was on themselves and their well-being and not those outside their class. When they did approach socioeconomic issues, it was with lukewarm attention. In their hearts, they really preferred to overlook social and economic concerns because it didn't affect them like it did the poor and the oppressed. But, to show some degree of identification with Christ for public relations reasons, they lukewarmly mentioned it in a sermon given to a charity but never threw their full weight and resources behind correcting the causes of socioeconomic injustice.

But Jesus took the temperature of the Laodicean church and spoke about them in three temperatures: hot, cold, and lukewarm. Jesus said,

> "I know your works, that you are neither cold nor hot. I would that you were cold or hot. So then, because you are lukewarm and neither cold nor hot, I will spit you out of My mouth. Because you say, 'I am rich, have become wealthy, and have need of nothing'—and do not know that you are wretched, miserable, poor, blind, and naked."

---

3. William R. Jones, "Purpose and Method in Liberation Theology: Implications for an Interim Assessment," in Deane Williams Ferm, ed, *Liberation Theology, North American Style* (New York: Verizon, 1987), 156–157.

Notice here that Jesus not only took the temperature of this church, but he made it clear that they did not know they were spiritually sick. They had walking pneumonia and did not know it. They were critically ill and needed ICU attention but didn't know it. Jesus said you don't know you are "Wretched, miserable, poor, blind, and naked." The Laodicean church was lukewarm. They had the wrong temperature to be a church. They were lukewarm. Lukewarm means timid, lacking conviction, halfhearted, and not excited.

Due to the spiritual temperature of this church and their lack of paying attention to its temperature, Jesus rejected this church by spitting it out of his mouth. Too many churches don't have the right temperature. They have become lukewarm. They preach lukewarm sermons, sing lukewarm songs, pray lukewarm prayers, have lukewarm ministries, give lukewarmly, and have a lukewarm commitment toward the Kingdom of God. No wonder they put everything else first before the Kingdom of God. They don't have the right temperature. Prayer meetings and Bible studies are not a priority for them. Other interests are more important than spiritual knowledge and growth. This is why the world cannot distinguish between Christians and non-Christians. They cannot tell who are children of God and who are children of the devil. So many Christian people are acting the same, if not worse, than people of the world.

Jesus prefers a church to be cold or hot but never lukewarm. This begs the question: what is a cold church? A cold church is doing what it wants to do without regard to the Word of God. It is like Burger King, "Have it your way." Too often people want to be Christians on their terms and do it their way. They want to follow Jesus Christ on our terms, creating all kinds of rationalizations and interpretations to set up discrimination in which people cannot experience true liberation. It supports cultural norms regardless of how these norms don't square with the Word of God. A cold church is narrow-minded, racist, sexist, etc. and doesn't care what others think. They only think and operate in terms of what they believe even though their beliefs are far from the Kingdom of God. For example, when Kenneth Cauthen, a theology professor at Colgate Rochester Divinity, was a baptist pastor in the state of Georgia and supported the Supreme Court's decision outlawing segregation in public schools, he sent letters to the Atlanta newspaper concurring with the decision. Some of his members were angry with him and made provisions to have him dismissed as pastor. Cauthen described how coldhearted church people could be when he took a stand against religious and educational bigotry. This church did not consider the social sins of which they were participating by fighting against the supreme court ruling that segregation in public schools was unconstitutional. Cauthen talked about his experience.

> Eventually, I got into trouble over the stand I took. In particular, some members were incensed over some letters I wrote to the Atlanta newspaper, along with a sermon I preached. The chairman of the Board of Deacons came to tell me that an effort was underway to have me removed from my office as pastor. He had refused to meet with the deacons to consider the issue unless I was present. He had come to invite me to the meeting. We engaged in a lengthy discussion, during which I appealed to the Scriptures as the basis for my judgments about race. In anger, he said, "I don't care what the Bible says; we are not going to permit the integration of the races in our schools."[4]

A cold church doesn't care what the scriptures say. Although the Word of Christ is spirit and life (John 6:63) and should be the authority in our decision-making process, many Christians don't care what it says. They only care for their tradition and cultural norms, and if the scriptures can embellish these norms, fine, but when they challenge these norms, they dump them like a hot potato. They want to advance their agenda and not the Kingdom of God. This is the overall practice of American Christianity. They know what the scriptures say about injustice and inequality, but they ignore it and practice another type of Christianity, which is out of alignment with the Christianity of Christ.

It is amazing how many pastors can point out other sins like alcohol consumption, gambling, pornography, adultery, greed, homosexuality, and materialism but fail to point out the social sins of racism and injustice. They are morally blind when it comes to social sin. "As long as [they see] in our present society only a few inevitable abuses and recognizes no sin and evil deep-seated in the very constitution of the present order, [they are] still in

---
4. Kenneth Cauthen, *I Don't Care What the Bible Says* (Mercer University Press, 2003), x–xi.

a state of moral blindness and without conviction of sin."[5] Many pastors skip over social justice while preaching about individual piety. Although many of their members may subscribe to tenets of white supremacy, they dare not preach about it because such a controversial message may upset the good-paying members of the church. They don't understand that the sin that won't be confessed is the sin that cannot be conquered. God cannot forgive a sin people won't admit having. Jeremiah said to the people of Israel, "Only acknowledge your guilt (Jeremiah 3:13)." Because too many pastors are afraid to acknowledge . . . problems in the church, the socioeconomic structures are maintained. It is disheartening that many pastors are afraid to challenge the temperature of their churches for the cause of Jesus Christ. "They play everything safe, preach only on subjects that never reach the level of controversy, and cuddle up to their members, their boards, and the powers-that-be in the hope of enjoying an untroubled and prosperous senescence."[6] Too many pastors have betrayed their calling and sold the truth of God for economic and political pottage. Walter Rauschenbusch stated:

> A minister has no business to be the megaphone of a political party and its catchwords. He should rather be the master of politics by creating the issues which parties will have to espouse. . . . It is the business of a preacher to connect all that he thinks and says with the mind and will of God, to give the religious interpretation to all human relations and questions, and to infuse divine sympathy and passion into all moral discussions. If he fails in that, he is, to that extent, not a minister of religion. . . . If a man sacrifices his human dignity and self-respect to increase his income or stunts his intellectual growth and his human affections to swell his bank account, he is to that extent serving mammon and deny God.[7]

Jesus has already made it clear that "No one can serve two masters; for either he will hate the one and love the other, or else he will be loyal to the one and despise the other. You cannot serve God and mammon (Matthew

---

5. Walter Rauschenbusch, *Christianity and the Social Crisis*, 349.
6. Bruce Catton's, *The Human Problems of the Minister*, by Daniel D. Walker, (New York, Evanston, and London: Harper & Row, 1960), 146.
7. Walter Rauschenbusch, *Christianity And The Social Crisis*, 362–69.

6:24)." It is difficult, if not impossible, to transform society without the assistance of the clergy, but when the clergy have become morally blind and have no conviction of sin, the social order drifts farther and farther away from the transforming power of the Kingdom of God. Too often, clergy and congregations want to be Christians on their terms and do it their way. They want to follow Jesus Christ on their terms, creating all kinds of rationalizations and interpretations that set up discrimination in which people cannot experience true spiritual, socioeconomic liberation. Harry Emerson Fosdick said, "In the church, we pray that the world may be saved, but commonly when we leave the church, we still try to save the world without changing it. Many Americans today would love to save the world if only they could save it without changing their isolationism, without changing their ideas of absolute national sovereignty, without changing their racial prejudices and their economic ideas to fit the interdependent world."[8] This is not only the case with issues of racism and oppression but other issues like same-sex marriage, which is clearly not the Will of God. If the church does not challenge the culture with the gospel of Jesus Christ, then who will? If the church cannot conquer culture, culture will conquer the church by casting its spell over the moral judgment of the church.

Simply put, a cold church is a cultural church that approves ungodly practices regardless of what the Bible says. This is a church that talks about grace, but it is a cheap grace that frustrates the will of God. It is a grace by which people have not died to themselves and come alive in Jesus Christ. It is a church that refuses to take up its cross and follow Jesus Christ. As long as the budget is met and the staff is paid, don't challenge the temperature of the church; don't rock the boat—although the boat is spiritually sinking—leave controversial issues like racism alone, and time will work things out. American Christianity has had 401 years to get rid of racism, at least among Christians, but time has only caused it to get worse. Too many American Christians can be described in the words of Richard Niebuhr, "We want a Christ without a cross, a church without discipline, a God without wrath, a Kingdom without judgment."[9] At least Jesus knows the

---

8. Harry Emerson Fosdick, *Answers to Real Problems: Harry Emerson Fosdick Speaks To Our Time*, edited by Mark E. Yurs (Wipf & Stock, 2008), 178.

9. H. Richard Niebuhr, cited from *Black Church Lifestyles, Rediscovering the Black Christian Experience*, compiled by Emmanuel L. McCall (Nashville, TN: Broadman Press, 1986), 161.

stance of a cold church and prefers it to a lukewarm one. At least Jesus knows a cold church stands in active opposition to His Word, and it makes no apology for endorsing things that would not be tolerated in the Kingdom of God. Jesus knows a cold church is callous towards the Kingdom of God and its righteousness, callous towards racial justice, callous towards equality, and obeying and participating in the ministry of reconciliation. Jesus knows how to deal with a cold church because they are not pretending to be anything else but what and who they are.

The same is true for a hot church. A hot church is on fire and spiritually and physically involved in matters of faith to do God's will without apology. It is not interested in trying to be in step with the culture nor square with some political platform. When the social order is out of moral order, a hot church filled with the Holy Spirit lovingly speaks the truth but is ready for the consequences of speaking that truth. This kind of church is prepared to lay down its life for the cause of Christ. This church works to be a thermostat to set the temperature of society instead of being a thermometer that registers the temperature of society. It works to bring into existence the Kingdom of God on earth and understands, "It is better to obey God rather than men (Acts 5:29)." Whatever the cost to help usher in God's reign on earth, a hot church is willing to pay the price. Which means it is ready to practice civil disobedience to uphold the truth of the Kingdom of God.

For example, after the religious establishment ordered Peter, James, and the apostles not to teach nor preach in Jesus's name, they were beaten for disobeying this order, but they went away rejoicing, counting it worthy to suffer shame for his name (Acts 5:41). They and others were on fire, and the early Christian movement is the model of what it means to be a hot church in a cold and ungodly society. This does not mean this type of church hides behind stained glass windows and stands on the sideline while wrong, evil, and injustice spread its tentacles like a green-bay tree throughout society. This church does not avoid controversy; it inevitably enters conflict in a world already in conflict with the Kingdom of God. During the times of the early church, "Christianity did not spread only sweet peace and tender charity, but the leaven of social unrest. It caused some to throw down their tools and quit work. It stiffed women to break down the restraints of custom and modesty. It invaded the intimacies of domestic relations and threatened families with disruption. It awakened the slaves to a sense of worth and a longing for freedom, which made slavery doubly irksome and stained their relations with their masters. It disturbed the patriotism and loyalty of citizens for their country and intervened between the sovereign State and its subjects."[10] This type of church ultimately influenced a gladiatorial, blood thirsty, sexual deviant, oppressive, infanticide, and war-prone empire to become a Christian empire. Persecution could not stop them; imprisonments could not dissuade them; deaths could not deter them, and criticism could not divert them. They were a colony of Holy Spirit-filled disciples of Christ who knew in whom they believed. This is the type of church Christ prefers, one that is not trying to win the approval of a political platform, a social organization, or an economic system of some sort but focusing on carrying out the Will of God on earth as it is in heaven, whatever the cost.

However, the church that nauseates and sickens the Lord is a lukewarm church. The Lord hates such a church because its people cannot be dependent upon it. At a most needful hour when Christ needs a church to rise and shine, this church deflects and hides and makes excuses for its cowardice. It does not want to offend. It is a church that sits on the fence and cannot make up its mind about which side to stand on. It has a split loyalty. When it is safe, it gives Jesus Christ a little loyalty, but when it is not safe, it gives the world a little loyalty. This church sits at the Lord's table and also at the devil's table. It is trying to strike a balance between the Kingdom of this world and the Kingdom of God. It is a "both-and" church that Christ cannot stomach. Because it is lukewarm, Christ is about to spit it out of His mouth. The Laodicean church knew actually what the Lord was talking about because it was a city in which cool water came from one direction and hot water came from another direction and when it arrived in the city of Laodicea, it was warm. The analogy Jesus uses is to point out that the Laodicean church is lukewarm; they are straddles who cannot make of their minds to whom they will give their full allegiance. This church was financially stable, materially abundant, socially accepted, and politically connected. All of this to their credit was also to their detriment. Satan had blinded them. What this church considers success, Jesus sees it as failure; what this church sees as doing well Jesus sees it as sickness; what this church believes to be important, Jesus sees it as trivial. What this church believes to be relevant, Jesus sees it as irrelevant. The good

---

10. Walter Rauschenbusch, *Christianity And The Social Crisis*, 139.

reputation this church thought it had Jesus condemned it. This church was pleased with itself in what it had accomplished. Jesus was displeased with what it could have accomplished. Clovis G. Chappell stated why:

> Not only does Christ hate lukewarmness because it is hateful in itself, but because it robs its victims of all possibility of progress. This is true because warmness is a child of self-satisfaction. . . . The members of this church were well satisfied, they were content with themselves. They said: "We are rich and increased in goods and have need of nothing. They had all the knowledge of God, and all the spiritual power, and all the usefulness that they cared to have. They were sure that they had arrived. . . . For if you know as much as you want to know, you will not likely learn any more. If you are as good as you want to be, you will not get any better. If you are as high up the hill as you care to be, you will not climb any higher. If you are winning the world to Christ as rapidly as you want to win it, you will certainly not enlarge your efforts.[11]

This church reached a point where they didn't need Christ's help anymore because they depended on their own efforts. They had the resources; they had the education; they had the right connections. They no longer felt a need to be totally committed to the tenets of Christianity, and therefore, they embraced the culture and its definitions of success. Money, materialism, and method became more important to them than the message and mission of Jesus Christ and His Kingdom. Therefore, they were lukewarm towards Christ and the ministry of reconciliation.

By and large, this church represents American Christianity. Due to the wealth and power of the United States, there are many churches connected to the power structure of which they have been able to reach the heights of economic, social, and political respectability but, at the same time, lukewarm about bringing to bear the principles of the Kingdom of God upon the unjust social and economic structures. They think of themselves as Christians but support the unjust structures that favor the rich while punishing the poor. Even poor whites who are made poor by the same unjust socioeconomic structures as poor blacks vote to put in authority white leaders who refuse

---

11. Clovis G. Chappell, *Sermons on Old and New Testaments Characters* (Harper & Row, 1953), 72–73.

to come under the total authority of Christ. They, too, are caught between allegiance to color and to Christ. The white and black evangelical church must reconcile the two possibilities where they cannot completely condemn the structures of which they have achieved success, nor can they completely support the structures because of how the structures disfavor the poor. The church constantly lives with this conflicting duality, and unless the church decides between the two and throws its full weight and resources behind one or the other, they are as lukewarm as the Laodicean church of which Jesus Christ condemns by spitting it out of His mouth.

It is the hope of Christ and His Kingdom that the postmodern church repents and comes out of its centuries-long lukewarm posture and side with the Kingdom of God. The church is either with Christ or against Christ—the last hope for a world that's on the fringe of destroying itself. Racism and oppression carry the seed of its destruction. In order to conquer the world for Christ, the church must throw off the magic spell of the present order and come under the transforming power of the Kingdom of God. It cannot be married to Christ but in the bed with the oppressors of the world. The church is either for Christ or against Christ. It cannot be both. Rauschenbusch said, "We must repent of the sins of existing society, cast off the spell of the lies protecting our social wrongs, have faith in a higher social order, and realize in ourselves a new type of Christian manhood which seeks to overcome the evil in the present world, not by withdrawing from the world, but revolutionizing it."[12] No one knows how long we have to Christianize our world with the Christianity of Christ. The signs point to the fact that we don't have long. What Jesus Christ pointed out in the scriptures is being fulfilled before our very eyes. We can ignore the signs and continue business as usual and run the risk of being spit out of the mouth of the Savior, or take the remaining time and use it for the work and ministry of the Kingdom of God. One thing is sure: a lukewarm church cannot remain in Jesus Christ. It may remain in a social and economic system; it may remain in a political state and in a religious cluster of churches, but as far as Christ is concerned, this church is vomit and will be spit out of the mouth of the Savior. Translation: this church will lose its soul unless it repents and moves out of its lukewarm posture.

---

12. Walter Rauschenbusch, *Christianity And The Social Crisis*, 412.

Chapter Nine
CULTURAL CHRISTIANS

Saying no to flag worship dethrones the American Jesus and it exposes our cultural Christianity. —David D. Flowers

To understand cultural Christians, we need to understand what culture is and how this creates tension between Christians and culture. A simple definition of culture is the way people agree to live out their lives in human society, and this is not to exclude religion, which undergirds culture. Paul Tillich said, "Religion is the substance of culture; culture is the form of religion."[1] Tillich is saying that at the heart of culture is religion. H. Richard Niebuhr carries the definition further. He stated that "Culture is the artificial, secondary environment which man superimposes on the natural. It comprises language, habits, ideas, beliefs, customs, social organizations, inherited artifacts, technical processes, and values. . . . the world of culture is a world of values."[2] These values are ground rules on how people agree to behave in society based on their fundamental beliefs that guide or inform their actions. Cultural values are what we believe to be our highest good. Cornel West stated, "Culture is as much a structure as the economy or politics; it is rooted in institutions such families, schools, churches, synagogues, mosques, and communication industries (television, radio, video, music). Similarly, the economy and politics are not only influenced by values but also promote particular cultural ideas of the good life and good society."[3]

---
1. Paul Tillich, *Theology of Culture* (London: Oxford University Press, 1969), 42.
2. H. Richard Niebuhr, *Christ And Culture* (New York: Harper & Row, 1951), 32–34.
3. Cornel West, *Race Matters* (New York: Vintage Books, A Division of Random House, Inc., 1993), 19.

Given this definition, we can see how culture can and often does create conflict and tension for Christians. If there is no conflict, there is collaboration, and where there is collaboration, there is no conversion. For example, one of the cultural values of the people of Rome was Caesar. No other law or person should be elevated above Caesar. This created tension and conflict for early Christians. Since Christians are in the world but not of the world, what are they to do when cultural values work at cross purposes with the teachings of Jesus Christ? It is either Caesar or Christ. It is either the Roman Empire or the Kingdom of God. The choice Christians have is either live in line with culture or live counterculture. Since the life of Jesus Christ was against culture, especially when it interfered with the values of the Kingdom of God, He practiced counterculture and expects His followers to do no different. The culture of this world and the culture of the Kingdom of God are in conflict, and no follower of Jesus Christ can live in line with both.

Since culture is what humans create, then the American culture is a creation of the white power structure. This cultural structure puts the white elite on the top and everyone else on the bottom. The elite has so constructed society as to divide the human family into alleged superior and inferior categories. For example, male, female; white, black; rich, poor; master, slave; educated, uneducated; in-group, out-group—are some of its familiar examples. This hierarchical arrangement must not only be a strategy to divide and conquer but interpreted as sacrosanct against all opposition. This means these created inequalities must be taught to the poor, the oppressed, and the marginalized so that this hierarchical arrangement is in line with the order of the universe, and those at the bottom of this arrangement are actually serving their highest good by accepting it as the Will of God. As long as this is taught, accepted, and reinforced by the political power players, this maintains an unequal distribution of wealth, power, and privileges. When this arrangement is challenged, the power players, with the silence and complicity of the Christian church, unleash violence upon the challengers and brand them as bad, evil, and unpatriotic to discourage the increase of challengers. It is better to deal with a few challengers of the cultural structures and crush them than with many challengers. One thing oppressors don't want is the exposing of their created cultural structures that benefit only them. They must keep these structural creations as invisible as possible by assigning them to a sacred frame of reference outside its human creation. When people are made to believe that the social and economic structures are God's creation in human society, people are less likely to challenge it and build their lives around accepting it. When people start to question the cultural structures as human creation and not God's creation, the human creators don't mind employing the power of violence to keep this cultural system protected.

Paulo Freire stated, "Violence is initiated by those who oppress, who exploit, who fail to recognize others as persons—not by those who are oppressed, exploited, and unrecognized. It is not the unloved who initiate disaffection, but those who cannot love because they love only themselves."[4] Violence is automatically the result of the system of oppression, and its militarism should not be underestimated in the quest for liberation. Coming to the end of his life, Martin Luther King, Jr. realized that powerlessness is the creation of the cultural elites to keep the slums and ghettos intact. Because Martin Luther King, Jr. demonstrated countercultural actions, he was persecuted, threatened, and harassed by those who wanted no change in the cultural structures. King said, "The plantation and the ghetto were created by those who had power both to confine those who had no power and to perpetuate their powerlessness. The problem of transforming the ghetto is, therefore, a problem of power—a confrontation between the forces of power demanding change and the forces of power dedicated to preserving the status quo."[5] These cultural structures have also duped the oppressed. Therefore, to reduce and eliminate socioeconomic injustice, we must engage in transforming the cultural and religious underpinning that holds it up. Religion and culture are so intertwined and woven together that it is difficult to transform one without affecting the other.

Cultural arrangements also have international implications where oppressors can live in one nation while taking advantage of other nations to increase their wealth, power, and privileges. With this understanding of how culture is created and how the creators of culture place themselves at the top of the socioeconomic heap, we can understand how racism is a by-product of

---

4. Paulo Freire, *Pedagogy of the Oppressed*, 37.
5. Martin Luther King, Jr., *The Radical King*, edited and introduced by Cornel West (Boston, MA: Beacon Press, 2015), 193.

such creation and how religion is utilized to maintain the cultural, structural arrangement. If American Christianity does not take under consideration the unjustness and unfairness of this hierarchal arrangement in society and does not work against it in some way, form, or fashion, they are no doubt cultural Christians. It is not enough to save souls for Christ when these souls live in neighborhoods and communities that are the direct result of social, economic, and ecological injustice. Cultural Christians are only concerned about getting souls into heaven, not about transforming the social arrangement in which these souls have to live out their lives. Robert McAfee Brown stated this is the heresy of modern Protestantism. They believe all you need to do is get people saved and then let them deal with the social order. This is like helping a disadvantaged pregnant woman deliver her baby and then leaving the woman and baby to fend for themselves, not taking into consideration the overwhelming socioeconomic condition they have to struggle to live in. McAfee Brown said:

> If we define evangelism as "sharing the good news," . . . It is clear that there are many ways in which the good news is shared. Calling individuals to decision is one of them, but it is not the only one, and it is unfortunate that individual decision has become the popular stereotype for the entire evangelistic venture. Indeed, modern Protestantism's particular heresy in this regard has been its insistence that evangelism is an individual business, so that it is enough to change individuals and then let them change society. But the evangelization of individuals is never enough. It takes a lifetime to convert even a small group of individuals, after which the process must begin all over again, while injustices of society are studiously being ignored. . . . To convert a man living in substandard housing without concern for the appalling conditions under which he must raise his family is to betray a deficient vision of the concerns of the gospel for that man's life. His "conversion" has not completed the evangelistic task. It has only gotten it properly launched.[6]

Of course, cultural Christians are not really concerned about ministering to the whole person. They want to keep the socioeconomic structures

---

6. Robert McAfee Brown, *The Spirit of Protestantism* (New York: Oxford University Press, 1961), 203.

the way they are. They want to keep apart individual concerns and political concerns when salvation includes both. They know that "Politics determines who gets bread and who starves, who gets justice and who does not, who votes, and who goes to jail."[7] One of the major reasons Jesus will say to cultural Christians, "Depart from me," is they never widen the circle to minister to the whole person to work against structural injustice and its religious legitimation. Cultural Christians never take up a cross to follow Christ and are only concerned about the souls of people, but not the socioeconomic structures that trap souls in unjust conditions. They have symbols of the cross, but they won't bear the cross to do what needs to get done to bring about the reign of the Kingdom of God in human society. As long as Christian principles support their peaceful lifestyles, cultural Christians are not interested in "Comforting the afflicted and afflicting the comfortable." It is easy to be a Christian as long as this doesn't involve confronting the powers that be about wrong, evil, and injustice. They don't mind praying about unjust situations, but they are not going any further than this. Cultural Christians go along to get along, and whatever the culture comes up with next—for peace's sake, they adjust their theology and worldview accordingly. They refuse to distinguish between the sacred and the secular. As long as people are nice and polite, cultural Christians tolerate sin and immorality without a moral outcry. They see reality through the lens of the culture, not through the lens of biblical scripture. Their first defense is it's about love. They talk as if love cannot be twisted and distorted to support whatever people want to do. Oppressors and racists can enslave and marginalize people in the name of loving their country.

Moreover, many evangelical churches don't mind giving out Bibles but they fail to do what is written in the Bible. David Walker spoke about Bibles in the hands of white Americans back in the 19th century. He wrote, "Have not the Americans the Bible in their hands? Do they believe it? Surely, they do not. See how they treat us in open violation of the Bible!"[8] This is the reason Frederick Douglass railed against missionaries who wanted to give Bibles to the slaves. Douglass said:

---

7. ibid., 203.
8. David Walker, "Our Wretchedness in Consequence of the Preachers of Religion," cited from *Afro-American Religious History A Documentary Witness*, edited by Milton C. Sernett (Durham, NC: Duke University Press, 1985), 191.

> First, give us ourselves, and then we will get Bibles. What the slave begs for is his freedom, and the American and Foreign Anti-Slavery Society comes forward and says, 'Here is a Bible . . .' For my part, I am not for giving the slave the Bible or anything else this side of his freedom. Give him that first, and then you need not give him anything else. He can get what he needs. . . . Now, what we want is to first give the slave himself. God did not say to Moses 'Tell my people to serve me that they may go free,' but 'God and tell Pharaoh to let my people go that they may serve me.' The first thing is freedom. It is the all-important thing. There can be no virtue without freedom—there can be no obedience to the Bible without freedom.[9]

Douglass understood oppressed and marginalized people wanted freedom and justice first. Before there is any talk about reconciliation, love, and forgiveness, oppressed people need justice first. Douglass also pointed out how babies were being sold to purchase Bibles for poor heathens, a total contradiction and the height of hypocrisy of American Christianity. Cultural Christians want to talk about love, reconciliation, and all of the platitudes of religion but steer away from justice, equality, and dignity. Isn't this what Jesus said to the Pharisees, "Woe to you Pharisees, because you give God a tenth of your mint, rue and all other kinds of garden herbs, but you neglect justice and the love of God. You should have practiced the latter without leaving the former undone (Luke 11:42)." Cultural Christians skip over God's denunciation of racism and injustice and focus on God's grace, forgiveness, and salvation. They never link their cultural Christianity with institutional structures as part of the major reason we have such a divided nation and segregated churches based on skin color. They never see their hands are the same guilty hands that crucified Christ on the cross. Cultural Christianity, "That is a Christianity which surrenders its leadership to the social forces of national and economic life, offers no hope to the divided world. Lacking an integrating ethics lacking a universal appeal, it continues to follow the fortunes of the world, gaining petty victories in a war it has long lost. From it, the world can expect none of the prophetic guidance it requires in its search for synthesis."[10]

---

9. Frederick Douglass, *The Life and Writings of Frederick Douglass*, vol. 2, edited by Philip S. Foner (New York: International Publishers, 1975), 182–83.
10. H. Richard Niebuhr, *The Social Sources of Denominationalism*, 275.

To satisfy their conscience, cultural Christians don't mind worshipping together with members of the oppressed, swapping pulpits, attending conferences with them, and coming together for church programs. This is tolerated as long as the socioeconomic power dynamics between the two remain the same. But, when it seems like there may be a socioeconomic power shift, it strains the fellowship, and soon, the schism becomes visible again. They display a strange forgetfulness of how the nation became a superpower on the backs of the oppressed, and it is the duty of followers of Christ to help right this historical wrong. Yet, nationalism, racism, and political sectarianism are more important than the new patriotism that could be achieved in Jesus Christ. Cultural Christians have no interest in transforming the structural arrangement of society. Therefore, we should not expect them to give up their gods of socioeconomic privilege, power, superiority, and those things they hold dear to their hearts. They cannot conceive of giving all of this up to follow Jesus because, as the rich man who had great wealth, it is too much to sacrifice (Luke 12:33). Gaining and possessing are the stock and trade of cultural Christianity.

This type of culture not only gives oppressors the outcome they desire but this type of culture also affects the oppressed as well. The oppressed fight against self-abnegation by getting caught up in the culture of consumption to feel they have worth in human society. When the oppressed look at the power, wealth, and material possessions of the oppressor, they desire these material gains as well. The middle and upper-class African Americans can acquire these material possessions, but the lower class find themselves desiring these things sometimes by fighting and killing each other to acquire them. The images of success are very seductive for the oppressed regardless of what socioeconomic class they are in, and this causes many of them to become cultural Christians. It is cash, comfort, and convenience over Jesus Christ. Cornel West stated,

> "African Americans are influenced greatly by the images of comfort, convenience, machismo, femininity, violence, and sexual stimulation that bombard consumers. These seductive images contribute to the predominance of the market-inspired way of life over all others and thereby edge out non-market values—love, care, service to

others—handed down by preceding generations. The predominance of this way of life among those living in poverty-ridden conditions, with a limited capacity to ward off self-contempt and self-hatred, results in the possible triumph of the nihilistic threat in black America."[11]

The prosperity gospel has embellished the desire for material possessions, and a large percentage of white and black churches are advancing a culture of materialism.

As indicated earlier, religion is one of the major props that serve the maintenance needs of an unjust social arrangement and one of the major reasons this arrangement is not justly rearranged. Some people think we must totally get rid of religion to transform social arrangements for justice and equality. We don't have to get rid of religion because it is intertwined with culture, as Richard Niebuhr pointed out. We need to get rid of a particular type of religion that undergirds unjust cultural arrangements. Cultural Christianity is a prime example of a religion we must get rid of because it supports unjust cultural arrangements instead of challenging them. Cultural Christianity is really America's civil religion that promotes the allegiance to the flag, allegiance to the 'American Way of Life' and all the cultural ideologies that fuse God, country, and the flag in one whole synthesis. This allegiance is the reason we cannot solve racial injustice, police brutality, and poverty. Until cultural Christians shift their allegiance from civil religion to the Christianity of Christ, religion in America will continue to be a sham. Russel D. Moore tells how disenchanted he became with cultural Christianity and the questions it provoked within him:

> The cultural Christianity around me seemed increasingly artificial and cynical and even violent. I saw some Christians who preached against profanity use jarring racial epithets. I saw a cultural Christianity that preached hellfire and brimstone about sexuality, immorality, and cultural decadence. And yet, in the church where the major tither was having an affair everyone in the community knew about, there he was, in our neighbor congregation's "special music" time, singing "If It Wasn't for That Lighthouse, Where Would This Ship Be?" I saw a cultural

---
11. Cornel West, *Race Matters*, 26–27.

Christianity with preachers who often gained audiences, locally in church meetings or globally on television, by saying crazy and buffoonish things, simply to stir up the base and to gain attention from the world. . . . I saw a cultural Christianity cut off from the deep theology of the Bible and enamored with books and audio and sermon series tying current events to Bible prophecy. . . . Even as a teenager, I could recognize that the issues just happened to be the same as the talking points of the Republican National Committee. . . . But why was there a "Christian" position on congressional term limits, a balanced budget amendment, and the line item veto? Why was there no word on racial justice and unity for those of us in the historical shadow of Jim Crow?[12]

It is untenable to talk about racial injustice in a culture that created it, maintains it, and condoles it. Cultural Christians would rather guide the minds of their supporters away from issues of race and justice to talk about Jesus, who paid the price for sin, as if the sin of racism doesn't presently exist. It is easier to talk about a Jesus who was meek and mild than a Jesus who was radical and turned the tables over and ran money changers out of the temple. Cultural Christians are very selective in using scriptures to support what they are doing than those scriptures that really challenge them to repent from the socioeconomic sins they are yet involved in. If racial justice and equality are not part of the religious equation, then cultural Christians must understand that out of all they do; the worship services they have, the conventions and seminars they hold, the revivals they give around the country and the world, not any of this is acceptable to God. Why? Because God spoke through the prophet Amos, saying these words,

> "I hate, I despise your religious festivals; your assemblies are a stench to me. Even though you bring me burnt offerings and grain offerings, I will not accept them. Though you bring choice fellowship offerings, I will have no regard for them. Away with the noise of your songs! I will not listen to the music of your harps. But let justice roll on like a river, righteousness like a never-failing stream (Amos 5:21-24)."

---

12. Russell D. More, *"Can The Religious Right Be Saved?"* Firstthings.com, The 2016 Erasmus Lecture, January 2017.

God is making it abundantly clear that justice is a required coefficient in human and divine relations. There can be no vertical relationship with God when the horizontal relationship is devoid of justice. This is the reason Black Lives Matter continues to chant, "No justice, no peace." God is saying the same thing from heaven: "No justice, no peace with God." Mark O. Hatfield saw the difference between America's allegiance to civil religion than to the Christianity of Christ and the desperate need to repent. In a prayer breakfast back in 1973, he gave some biting but truthful words to his hearers that need repeating today:

> My brothers and sisters, as we gather at this prayer breakfast, let us beware of the real danger of misplaced allegiance, if not outright idolatry, to the extent that we fail to distinguish between the god of an American civil religion and the God who reveals himself in the holy Scriptures and in Jesus Christ. If we as leaders appeal to the god of civil religion, our faith is in a small and exclusive deity, a loyal spiritual adviser to power and prestige, a defender of only the American nation, the object of a national folk religion devoid of moral content. But if we pray to the biblical God of justice and righteousness, we fall under God's judgment for calling upon his name but failing to obey his commands. Our Lord Jesus Christ confronts false petitioners who disobey the Word God: 'Why do you call me 'Lord, Lord' and do not the things I say?" (Luke 6:46). God tells us that acceptable worship and obedience are expressed by specific acts of love and justice: Is not this what I require of you . . . to loose the fetters of injustice . . . to snap every yoke and set free those who have been crushed? Is it not sharing your food with the hungry, taking the homeless poor into your house, clothing the naked when you meet them, and never evading a duty to your kinsfolk? [Isa. 58:6-7]. We sit here today as the wealthy and the powerful. But let us not forget that those who follow Christ will more often find themselves not with comfortable majorities but with miserable minorities. Today, our prayers must begin with repentance.[13]

Hatfield understood that the majority of American Christians were cultural Christians with an allegiance to civil religion. Cultural Christians

---

13. Mark O. Hatfield, "The Sin That Scarred Our National Soul," *The Christian Century*, vol. XC, no. 8 (February 1, 1973), 221.

need to repent from their allegiance to civil religion because it promotes white supremacy, power, privilege, prosperity, and even violence; as our national anthem says, "And the rocket's red glare, the bombs bursting in air, gave proof through the night that our flag was still there." Cultural Christians are willing to give their endorsement of using bombs and drones to achieve national interests when those interests are not the interest of the Kingdom of God. The god of civil religion is not the God of Jesus Christ. Yet, many American pastors and politicians invoke God in their language about American prosperity and American exceptionalism as if these things had divine sanctions. Rosemary Radford Ruether, a feminist theologian, spoke about this in her writings:

> The problem of civil religion in the rhetoric of American politicians is not that of too much or too little God-talk, but of what kind. God-talk tends to be used by politicians to mystify social reality. We talk of God 'crowning our good with brotherhood from sea to shining sea.' This kind of language carries several assumptions (aside from the assumption that all Americans are "brothers"). It assumes that an idyllic social and physical community has already been established as our reality and heritage. It assumes that God is the author of American success; therefore, American success is basically natural, innocent and good. All this is social ideology with divine sanctions. It obscures a lot of our real history. We would never be allowed to mention that much of our prosperity has come from vicious exploration—of slaves, of workers, of the human labor and raw materials of many other parts of the globe. That brotherhood (let alone sister-brotherhood) does not reign from city to polluted city also is unmentionable. A rosy glow of utopia is imposed on our reality as the true American identity, blocking out critical thinking or making it "unpatriotic."[14]

Pushing past all the American mythology, Pauli Murray says that Rosemary Ruether further criticizes how American Christianity has "Become the cultural guardian of the symbols of domination and subjugation and

---

14. Rosemary Radford Ruether, "Mystification or Liberation?" *The Christian Century*, vol. XCIV, no.1 (January 5-12, 1977), 4.

this role is apostasy to the mission of the church. The Church must exorcise these demonic symbols within its structure and must recover its own revolutionary heritage as liberating force in the world."[15]

Mystification is a big feature of cultural Christianity. Instead of seeing reality as it really is concerning racism and oppression, cultural Christians paint a rosy picture that all is well in America. When they talk and preach about sin, it is communicated as personal problems with individuals, not social and economic problems. They talk about sin in crime-ridden areas where drugs, prostitution, and pregnancy are often the outcome. No doubt, these are areas of sin, but sin is also in affluent areas and places of power. Very rarely do cultural Christians talk about the sins at the top that cause a lot of the sins at the bottom, where poverty, poor education, and few opportunities are the circumstances of disadvantaged people. Harry Emerson Fosdick expands the concept of sin:

> We often deceive ourselves because sin can take such a high polish. Sometimes, sin is gross and terrible. It staggers down the street; it blasphemes with oaths that can be heard; it wallows in vice unmentioned by modest lips. Then prosperity visits sin. It moves to a finer residence; it seeks the suburbs or gets itself domiciled on a college campus. It changes all its clothes. It is no longer indecent and obscene; its speech is mild; its civility is irreproachable. But at heart, it is the same old sin, self-indulgent, callous, envious, cruel, unclean. As anybody may easily observe, sin takes on a very high polish. The tragedy in all of this is that my sin is not simply mine individually but may share in the corporate evil that is destroying the hopes of the world. For selfishness, carnality, cruelty, are not merely individual; they roll from generation to generation, spoiling all man's hopes, and my curse is that I can be part of this major problem of the race instead of part of the answer.[16]

I have yet to hear catholic and evangelical pastors preach about the social and economic sin of racism. If they do preach about it, it is a

---

15. Pauli Murray, "Black Theology And Feminist Theology: A Comparative View," cited from *Black Theology A Documentary History, 1966–1979*, edited by Gayraud S. Wilmore and James H. Cone, (Maryknoll NY: Orbis Books, 1979), 412.
16. Harry Emerson Fosdick, *Answers to Real Problems*, edited by Mark E. Yurs, 138–39.

one-time situation, possibly when something has happened like the death of George Floyd. and the pressure is on to say something about it. The reason is this type of preaching makes people uncomfortable, and when people are uncomfortable they tend not to give financially. Therefore, to keep the money coming in and the pews filled, cultural Christian pastors and preachers would rather speak on topics that never reach the level of controversy. What cultural Christians don't understand is we cannot heal what we fail to acknowledge and confess. When cultural Christianity hides its original sin and never acknowledges and repents of it, how can there be healing of the land? Ignoring a sickness won't heal it but will make it worse. God spoke centuries ago about how healing can take place in a land. "If My people who are called by My name will humble themselves, and pray and seek My face, and turn from their wicked ways, then I will hear from heaven, and will forgive their sin and heal their land (2 Chronicles 7:14)."

There was a confession of the sins of racism in 1973, but the strong undercurrents of racism kept the confession from developing into a national redemptive policy for the oppressed. A group of evangelicals confessed they had fallen short of social obligations and issued a Chicago Declaration that says the following:

> We acknowledge that we have failed to condemn the exploitation of racism at home and abroad by our economic system. . . . Before God and a billion hungry neighbors, we must rethink our values regarding our present standard of living and promote more just acquisition and distribution of the world's resources . . . We must challenge the misplaced trust of the nation in economic and military might—a proud trust that promotes a national pathology of war and violence which victimizes our neighbors at home and abroad. We must resist the temptation to make the nation and its institutions objects of near-religious loyalty. . . . We acknowledge that we have encouraged men to prideful domination and women to irresponsible passivity.[17]

Although there is an acknowledgment of the collective sin of racism and oppression, the next expected move is to correct the wrong, and this

---

17. Cited from *Religion in America*, 2nd Edition, George C. Bedell, Leo Sandon, Jr., Charles T. Wellborn, The Florida State University (New York: Macmillan Publishing Co., Inc., 1982), 335.

means restitution of some kind to remedy historical oppression, racism, and exploitation. Many cultural Christians fought against affirmative action that gives the oppressed people opportunities for social and economic uplift that they wouldn't otherwise have. Cultural Christians must repent and start being part of the solution rather than part of the problem. Real Christians are called to transform the culture and fashion it in such a way that we can move from historical sins to present-day brotherhood and sisterhood in Jesus Christ. Real Christians are called to proclaim the Kingdom of God and link the culture and its institutions to this Kingdom to serve God and bring glory to His name. In order to do this, cultural Christians must understand that being an almost Christian is not good enough. Cultural Christianity is not fully Christian, and this could cause cultural Christians to lose their souls while standing before the judgment seat of Christ. Unless cultural Christians move from their almost Christian status, they are sure to hear the words of the Savior, "Depart From Me."

I hope that cultural Christians see how dangerous it is to profess Christ and not possess Christ. Cultural Christians cannot get into the Kingdom of God by being almost Christian. When Paul was giving his life story before Paul's story so moved King Agrippa, he said to Paul, "Almost you persuaded me to be a Christian (Acts 26:28)." In other words, you almost persuaded me to follow Christ. You almost persuaded me to give up this life of power and prestige and follow Christ, but because of political and financial reasons Agrippa decided to remain as he is. He was convinced that Paul was right, but he decided not to be converted. Mental persuasion is not enough. To almost become a Christian is not enough. Agrippa was convicted, but he chose not to be converted. He was sure of the Excellency of the ways of God, but ego, position, power and prestige, and all of the cares of this world overruled his convictions. Therefore, Agrippa decided not to become a Christian. He decided to gain the world but lost his soul. This is the same problem we have with cultural Christians. Many of them are "almost" Christians. Almost is not good enough. Ninety-nine and a half won't do. God wants one hundred percent and more from his followers because Christ gave one hundred percent of Himself to save us in this world. Cultural Christians must first get saved to help save others. They must repent from their sins to challenge others to repent from theirs.

Paul says to cultural Christians, "You, then who teach others, do you not teach yourself? You who preach against stealing, do you steal? You who say that people should not commit adultery, do you commit adultery? You who abhor idols, do you rob temples? You who boast in the law, do you dishonor God by breaking the law? As it is written: 'God's name is blasphemed among the Gentiles because of you (Romans 2:21-24)."

Parenthetically, those who claim to be Christians and speak about democracy, do you keep others from benefiting from it? Those who claim God's justice, do you inflict injustice? Those who claim oneness in Christ, do you discriminate against others based on skin color? Those who say, "Love your neighbor," does this mean only those who look like you? Those who say, "One nation, under God, indivisible with liberty and justice for all," does this mean only the white race? Those who say America is a Christian nation, then why has the nation not "Loose the chains of injustice and untie the cords of the yoke, to set the oppressed free and break every yoke (Isaiah 58:6)?" If you say you are Christian, why practice cultural Christianity instead of the Christianity of Christ. Until American Christianity settles these questions in their hearts, they may be sure to hear "Depart from Me."

Chapter Ten
THERMOMETER CHRISTIANS

> *In those days, the church was not merely a thermometer that recorded the ideas and principles of popular opinion; it was a thermostat that transformed the mores of society.*
> —Martin Luther King, Jr.

After a thorough investigation of American Christianity, it is without doubt that most Christians in America are thermometer Christians. This conclusion is drown due to the unchanged socioeconomic structures and the unending results of injustice and inequality these structures produce. Until the unjust structures are truly dealt with and the focus of transformation is a top priority for American Christianity, changes will occur, but not corrections. When only changes are made, what is changed can reoccur. When corrections are made, what is corrected is permanent. In terms of the socioeconomic structures of America, only changes have been made, the rich and elite are still at the top of the social heap, and the poor and oppressed are still at the bottom. This situation of injustice and inequality will continue until true corrections are made.

Like cultural Christians, thermometer Christians don't affect corrections. They only record and embrace what is instead of what ought to be. They are either not interested in making corrections or too afraid because of the consequences of doing so. Nevertheless, the social order remains the same. History shows that thermometers Christians have carved out a place within the socioeconomic structure and are satisfied to live within these curved spaces. As long as they are unmolested by the powers that be, thermometer Christians are not interested in rocking the boat for justice, for equality, and for human dignity. Until they are serious about doing so, no systemic correction is possible in the American culture.

The reason we call many American Christians thermometers is they only reflect the temperature of society. When racism and oppression were in their infancy in America, those who considered themselves Christians did not set the temperature for the new republic but reflected its social and economic practices. It sided with the powerful against the powerless, and as a result, slavery lasted for two and a half centuries. Jim Crow lasted for one hundred years, and voting suppression is still a reality today. It is amazing how many thermometer Christians can talk about being one nation under God, indivisible, with liberty and justice for all, but yet reflect the very opposite of these words. They will vote for politicians who harbor racists and white supremacy ideology, making it difficult to transform the present socioeconomic structures of our nation. When some thermometer Christians are by themselves, they show certain niceties of respect and cordialness, but when they get around others who refuse to show this basic social etiquette, they won't show it either. They have learned to reflect on what is to survive living and coming into contact with different groups that hold different social and political views. Thermometer Christians know how to change their persona to fit the particular context they are in. If the situation requires them to be nice, they are nice, but when the situation requires them to be less nice, they are less nice. Thermometer Christians are comfortable sitting at the Lord's table as well as the devil's table. They are never consistent in their character, their attitude, and their sense of what is socially, economically, and morally right and wrong. They take on the persona of the majority opinion and follow the path of least resistance.

American Christianity has been and, in many respects, still is a disservice to the Kingdom of God in terms of racial justice and equality. It has not done all it could do to help break the stronghold of racism and oppression against black and brown people. Even now, when 43 states have 253 bills drafted to suppress the voting of black and brown people, it is predictable that thermometer Christians will sit back and allow it to happen, putting the nation back to the Jim Crows years. The question is, where is the outcry from the evangelical church? How many pastors have stood up in their pulpits or had a news conference to condemn this action when clearly this is taking the nation in the wrong direction? Again, thermometer Christians don't stand against the current but flow with it, right or wrong, just or unjust, moral or immoral, and this is one of the profound reasons America continues to descend into the abyss of despair. The old saying is, "If you don't stand for something, you will fall for anything."

American Christianity cannot correct injustice until it decides to move from its thermometer posture. It is often in the bed with the rich and powerful, who receive certain benefits for not going against the unjust race-based structures of society. Its legacy has been and continues to be a reflection of the larger society when it comes to race, justice, and equality. Jemar Tisby said, "A majority of white Christians refused to take a definitive stand against race-based chattel slavery, and this complicity plagued the church and created stark contradictions. Segregation and inequality defined most of American Christianity—even in an age of great revivals."[1] How can people hold religious services and revivals as though their contradictions and hypocrisy are not noticed by God? Better still, are people worshipping the God of Jesus Christ?

The god American Christianity worships is not the God of Jesus Christ because if it were, then their conscience would lay heavy with guilt, and the Holy Spirit would convict them to chart another course. Many American Christians confess that they are sorry for what happened to blacks and other people of color in the past, but their sorrow does not produce the courageous Christianity to correct the present socioeconomic structures. Could it be that they know the socioeconomic structures favor them over nonwhite people? It is difficult to transform a system when the wind is beneath your wings to airborne you into American success of wealth and power not understanding or caring that this same wind is contrary to the airborne of the oppressed. Thermometer Christians must understand that they cannot reflect the temperature of the Kingdom of this world and the Kingdom of Christ at the same time. Privately reflecting the Kingdom of God and publicly reflecting the Kingdom of this evil world won't stand

---

1. Jemar Tisby, *The Color of Compromise, The Truth About American Church's Complicity in Racism*, 68.

a chance before the judgment seat of Jesus Christ. They are sure to hear, "Depart from Me." This is no different than holding allegiance to America and the Soviet Union at the same time. People must make a choice which Kingdom they give their allegiance to. When America and the Soviet Union are in conflict and decide to go to war to resolve the conflict, people cannot be on both sides of the conflict. This is to say that the Kingdom of God and the Kingdom of this world are in conflict. We cannot be in both.

God required this decision for His chosen nation Israel. They were in the throes of indecision. Israel could not make up her mind which God to serve. They were undecided as to who is really God. Was it Baal or was it Yahweh? Israel drifted into apostasy; they were vacillating back and forth between the worship of God and the worship of Baal. Ahab the King allowed this kind of divided allegiance to fester in the land because his wife Jezebel introduced all kinds of false gods in the national life of Israel. This, however, led the people into idolatrous worship and practice. God required total devotion. The more Israel tried to synthesize the worship of God and the worship of Baal the farther away they drifted into idolatry. Israel was in a spiritual crisis. The nation could not survive under this kind of fickle climate. The worship of Baal and the worship of God could not co-exist. The nation had to make a choice. The story ends with God demonstrating through the prophet Elijah that He is the true and living God who demands total allegiance of His people (1 Kings 18:23). But, when His people try to serve God and other gods, God's prophet rises up to reprimand this synthesis.

Like Israel, American Christianity today must make a choice as to who is Lord of their lives. The culture around us has become so anti-God, so anti-morality, and intolerant that America has once again become a divided nation. The Civil War was a result over slavery, race and justice, and we have the same division today. Sadly, many people who considered themselves Christians were on the wrong side of history as they are today. We are called upon to decide. We have before us again the central unresolved issues of race, justice, and equality. We must decide what kind of nation we are going to be. We can't be thermostats and thermometers at the same time. It is not a "both and decision" but an "either or decision." We either choose God of Jesus Christ, or choose the lesser gods of life that will be the damnation of the soul of America. What is wrong with our world is not what sinners are doing, but what Christians are doing. Too many Christians are trying to serve God and the world. Some have turned away from the true and living God to serve the god of money, the god of pleasure, the god of gratification, the god of social prestige.

Many Christians are more concerned about status than about salvation. Some are more concerned about position and power than about justice and righteousness. These transitory gods we have created for ourselves are not able to save us. They are unreliable because they are not absolute, and since they are not absolute, they cannot be the "center of value." Wherever else our faith may be centered other than God; it cannot defend us against the void of meaninglessness. H. Richard Niebuhr stated, "All of our causes, all of our ideas, all the beings on which we relied to save us from worthlessness are doomed to pass."[2] This is to say that money, governments, philosophies, culture, social institutions are going to one day pass away and only God shall stand. The scripture says, "Whether there are prophecies, they shall fail; whether there are tongues, they shall cease; whether there is knowledge, it shall vanish away (1 Corinthians 13:8)." Hopefully, American Christianity will get it right this time as we struggle with race, racism, and the future of our nation.

To help in the process of moving American Christianity from its thermometer posture requires informed leadership. There is a lot of talk about how many of our leaders both civil and religious have lost touch with the people and the foundational values and principles that initially formed this great republic. Since leaders have lost touch with the people and with God, our nation is worse off. Nationally and internationally we are in a mess. There is a leadership crisis. We don't have enough leaders who have moral and spiritual vision, and who have convictions that cannot be swayed by the hostile winds of opposition. Look at our present day leadership in Washington, and how we don't have enough of them to stand amid committing political suicide to be the conscience of the nation. It is sad many of them are consensus leaders taking their direction from the Gallup polls. They are nothing more than thermometer leaders who just register the temperature of society.

---

2. H. Richard Niebuhr, *Radical Monotheism and Western Culture* (Louisville, KY: Westminster/John Knox Press, 1970), 122.

People have lost faith in many of our civic leaders because it seems they are more concerned about protecting their political and economic interest than they are about the interest of the nation. As thermometer leaders, they can find billions of dollars to fight a war that is still raging in Iraq but cannot find money to insure health care for millions of American citizens. They can support a tax break for the rich but cannot support a stimulus bill to help suffering citizens in their time of need. These days our leaders are for sale. Special interest groups come in and influence many of them and before you know it, "We the People" are holding the short end of the stick, if there is any stick left at all.

Many of our religious leaders are thermometer leaders as well. Religious leaders may not be responsible for legislating public policy, but they are called to influence public policy. They are called to speak truth to power. They are called to lift up their voices against evil, injustice, racism, oppression, exploitation and perversion in the land, and any leader afraid to speak up ought not to be a leader. They should keep in mind the words of Martin Niemoller:

> First they came for the Communists
> And I did not speak out
> Because I was not a Communist.
> Then they came for the Socialists
> And I did not speak out
> Because I was not a Socialist.
> Then they came for the trade unionists
> And I did not speak out
> Because I was not a trade unionist.
> Then they came for the Jews
> And I did not speak out
> Because I was not a Jew.
> Then they came for me
> And there was no one left
> To speak out for me.[3]

---

3. Martin Niemoller, "First They Came For the Socialists," United States Holocaust Memorial Museum. Retrieved 5 February, 2011.

There are too many timid leaders of the church. They are thermometer leaders just going around spreading sunshine and goodwill but never calling into question the unjust practices of the people and nation. These kinds of leaders have never affected positive social and economic changes in our world. It has always been the thermostat leaders who have helped to transform the world for the better. Cornel West's analysis of many of our present day leaders is spot on. He said many of them "Appear too hungry for status to be angry, too eager for acceptance to be bold, too self-invested in advancement to be defiant."[4] No church, no nation, and no kingdom needs thermometer leaders when we are in a time of crisis.

We need thermostat leaders like Shadrach, Meshach, and the Abednego who at the order of the King refused to bow before a golden image. We need leaders like Daniel who refused to stop praying at the decree of the King. We need leaders like Henry David Thoreau and Mahatma Gandhi who practiced civil disobedience in light of unjust laws. We need leaders like Abraham Lincoln who declared our nation cannot survive half slave and half free. We need leaders like Frederick Douglass, Martin Luther King, Jr., Malcolm X, Ella Baker, and Fannie Lou Hamer who were all voices and activists against wrong, evil, injustice, and inhumanity. We have too many thermometer leaders who are more concerned about basking in the light instead of being the light. Where are the prophetic voices of leaders who will speak what "Thus said the Lord?" The urgency of the times calls for leaders who are thermostats not thermometers.

Instead of being conscientious objectors, these court prophets were thermometers; they only registered what the King wanted. But, King Johoshaphat was not convinced, and he said to Ahab "Is there not here a prophet of the Lord, that we might inquire of him?" Is there a difference of opinion? Is there anybody else who is not in the same line of thought as these prophets you have in the court? Ahab said, "There is yet one man Micaiah, the son of Imlah, but I hate him for he does not prophesy good concerning me, but evil." I hate him because he always gives a different message that the court prophets give. I hate him because he doesn't tell me what I want to hear. I hate him because his "Thus said the Lord" messages don't set well with me. I have banished him from the court and condemned

---

4. Cornel West, *Race Matters*, 58.

him to prison. He is not a team player; he doesn't tell me what I want to hear. Although Micaiah was hated by King Ahab and put in prison, he was not going to be a thermometer prophet like the rest of the court prophets.

Micaiah demonstrated that he would be a nonconformist despite how unpopular this position might be. He decided to be a thermostat, a molder of society instead of being molded by society, and because of his convictions, his prophecy didn't square with the party platform of the ruling power. Micaiah was hated because he dared to be different; he spoke things that Ahab and his administration did not want to hear. He was jailed because he would not tone down and modify the message God had given him to speak. Due to his moral, ethical, and religious principles, Micaiah was not inducted into the hall of fame. He was not politically appointed to the court with the other 400 prophets who merely told the King what he wanted to hear. Of course this is what thermometer leaders do; they hang around people with power and say what the King wants to hear in order to keep their position of privilege.

But, Micaiah would not sell out; he had the moral courage and the spiritual backbone not to act like the rest; he stood for something, and we need leaders today who will stand for something greater than themselves; we need leaders who will stand on moral principles, justice, and equality for the good of the nation and the world. It has been said, "God doesn't want any coward soldiers in his army." When leadership demonstrate cowardice in the midst of a crisis, at a time when the better angels of our nature need to rise above the fray, and advocate for the Kingdom of Christ but do not, their actions weaken the church and they betray their calling. Too many Christian leaders have weakened the church and betrayed their calling. Not only is the cause in America, but it was the case when the Christian church in Germany knew about the persecution and genocide of the Jews but never opened their mouths against it. It is a sad fact but true that American Christianity is saturated with too many thermometer Christians, making it difficult if not impossible to get rid of institutional racism and oppressive structures that keep Christians divided and from reaching the goal of justice, equality, and a more perfect union.

Martin Luther King, Jr. was deeply disappointed in the white church during the struggle to desegregate the south. What he was dealing with is the same thing we are dealing with today; thermometer Christians. In his letter from the Birmingham jail King wrote these words:

> In spite of my shattered dreams of the past, I came to Birmingham with the hope that the white religious leadership of this community would see the justice of our cause, and with deep moral concern, serve as the channel through which our just grievances would get to the power structure. I had hoped that each of you would understand. But again I have been disappointed. . . . In the midst of blatant injustices inflicted upon the Negro, I have watched white churches stand on the sideline and merely mouth pious irrelevancies and sanctimonious trivialities. In the midst of a mighty struggle to rid our nation of racial and economic injustice, I have heard so many ministers say, "Those are social issues with which the gospel has no concern," and I have watched so many churches commit themselves to a completely otherworldly religion which made a strange distinction between body and soul, the sacred and the secular. . . . There was a time when the church was very powerful. . . . In those days the church was not merely a thermometer that recorded the ideas and principles of popular opinion; it was a thermostat that transformed the mores of society.[5]

It is no gainsaying that we as a nation are no closer to the reality of justice and equality than when King penned these words. American Christianity refuses to authentically shift from its thermometer posture to a thermostat posture. Until it is willing to do so, the racial division and enormous gap between the races will continue to get wider and wider and eventually destroy the republic.

In their investigation and analysis, Michael O. Emerson and Christian Smith came to this profound conclusion in their book called *Divided By Faith*:

> Despite devoting considerable time and energy to solving the problem of racial division, white evangelism likely does more to perpetuate the

---

5. Martin Luther King, Jr. "*Letter From the Birmingham City Jail,* April 16, 1963, cited from *A Testament of Hope,* edited by James Melvin Washington (Harper & Row, 1986), 299–300.

radicalized society than to reduce it. This, we have seen, is because of its history, its thorough acceptance of and reliance on free market principles, its subculture tool kit, and more broadly, the nature of the organization of American religion. . . . Most white evangelicals, directed by their cultural tools, fail to recognize the institutionalization of racialization—in economic, political, educational, social, and religious systems. They therefore often think and act as if these problems do not exist. As undetected cancer that remains untreated thrives and destroys, so unrecognized depths of racial division and inequality go largely unaddressed and likewise thrive, divide, and destroy. The solutions evangelicals propose and practice—though in many ways unique in modern America, and much needed as far as they go—simply cannot make much headway in the face of these powerful countercurrents that undercut and fight against their well intentioned, individualistic solutions.[6]

One could get depressed thinking this dilemma in America could last far in the future unless there is a radical transformation in the process. Because I firmly believe in the redemptive impulses of the Holy Spirit, it is my deep abiding faith that America can transform for the better. The transformation just may come through God's chosen remnant of white, black, brown, red, and yellow young people who are so filled with the fire of the Holy Spirit, they can never be identified as thermometers. They will be the glorious thermostats to achieve what many generations before have failed to accomplish. Unless there is a thermostat generation, American Christianity may hear the words of the Savior, "Depart from Me."

---

6. Michael O. Emerson, Christian Smith, *Divided By Faith, Evangelical Religion and the Problem of Race in America* (Oxford: Oxford University Press, 2000), 170.

CONCLUSION

Now all has been heard; here is the conclusion of the matter: Fear God and keep his commandments, for this is the duty of all mankind. —ECCLES. 12:13

The foregoing analysis of American Christianity shows that it has a lot of work to do to pass the Kingdom of God audit. If we had to give a grade to American Christianity based upon its historical and present practice, it has failed; failed to meet the demands of the Kingdom of Christ in a world full of evil, hate, injustice, and war. However, this doesn't mean there cannot be restoration after failure. The Judeo-Christian Bible is replete with examples of people and the nation of Israel that failed but was restored. Restoration came about after there was sincere repentance. To give up on American Christianity as hopeless is not to believe in redemption. This analysis of American Christianity was done to shed more light on its practice to vigorously encourage repentance before the Lord returns and pronounces judgment upon it. At this present stage, American Christianity is unacceptable to Christ and it should be unacceptable to us when we understand the life of Christ on earth and His teaching of the Kingdom of God.

If justice and equality are not coefficients within American Christianity, if there is abyssal silence about racism and oppression, police brutality, and exploitation of labor, then American Christianity is inauthentic. It is like what the Apostle Paul described as a "Sounding brass or a clanging cymbal (1 Corinthians 13:1)." There is no value to it that glorifies God, and this is the reason American Christianity has been viewed as a failure.

One of the greatest tragedies of American Christianity has been its failure to comprehend the physical as well as spiritual nature of human beings. With few exceptions, the church has attempted to address the spiritual needs of people while negating their physical and material requirements. Traditional theology has failed to see that ultimate salvation and historical liberation are inseparable aspects of the indivisible gospel of Jesus.[1]

Therefore, it is time for American Christianity to make a bold massive shift from its historical and present position to become the Christianity of Christ. The hope is in making the shift, and without choosing to make the shift, there is no hope to heal the racial divide. What is the Christianity of Christ? It is the very opposite of American Christianity of which we have love, justice, equality, dignity, forgiveness, reconciliation, and the constant affirmation of humanity. When people are more important than profit, faith is more important than fame, love is more important than luxury, principles are more important than power, and the willingness to carry a cross and die is more important than political party and property, we have the Christianity of Christ. Anything less than this fails the Holy Spirit test. The Christianity of Christ is about people, power, purpose, and provision. These are interrelated to achieve the will of God on earth as it is in heaven. How do we make the shift from American Christianity to the Christianity of Christ to have a better and different future than what we have had in the past?

First, we must go back and rediscover some very fundamental values that America has apparently lost. We must rediscover God. We must understand humanity comes from one blood. Without love we cannot make claims to Jesus Christ, and we need one another. These fundamental values are paramount in helping American Christianity make the transition to the Christianity of Christ. Martin Luther King, Jr. stated, "If we are to go forward, we must go back and rediscover these previous values—that all reality hinges on moral foundations and that all reality has spiritual

---

1. "Message to the Black Church and Community," National Conference of the Black Theology Project, in Atlanta, Georgia, August 3-7, 1977, cited in *Black Theology A Documentary History, 1966–1979*, edited by Gayraud S. Wilmore and James H. Cone, (Maryknoll, NY: Orbis Books, 1979), 346.

control."² We must go back and rediscover God who is the Creator of the universe. God is the One that sustains all life, and without Him we would certainly perish. Our view of God sets the gaze for our view of one another. If we don't respect God, we won't respect one another. Man's inhumanity to man is a direct disrespect for God. John said, "Whoever claims to love God yet hates a brother or sister is a liar. For whoever does not love their brother and sister, whom they have seen, cannot love God, whom they have not seen (1 John 4:20)."

This love for brother and sister goes beyond our immediate families; it encompasses the whole human race. We must rediscover the Fatherhood of God and the brother and sisterhood of mankind. J. I. Packer said, "If you want to judge how well a person understands Christianity, find out how much he makes of the thought of being God's child, and having God as his Father. If this is not the thought that prompts and controls his worship and prayers and his whole outlook on life, it means that he does not understand Christianity very well at all."³

Next, we must understand from one blood God made all nations of people (Acts 17:26). God did not make one race superior to another race. God did not make one race to rule other races. God made one human family and endowed the human family with gifts and talents to build His Kingdom on earth. So, to annihilate the lie that one color or race of people is superior to another, we need to rediscover that God made all of humanity out of the same matter and materials. All races have the same common thread running through their veins, which is red blood; and regardless of what our ethnic makeup is, everybody's blood is still red. We need to stop the pseudo-science that says because of the color of people's skin, they are naturally superior or inferior. We need to stop the false studies that say because of where people live, they are lacking in intelligence. A brain is a brain regardless of the its race, creed, or color.

There is no such thing as white or black supremacy. It doesn't matter if we are African, Indian, Asian, Englishman, Scotchman, Irishman, Norwegian, Frenchman, Italian, Russian, or whatever nationality we are. We are all related by one blood, and by one common ancestor without partiality.

---

2. Martin Luther King, Jr., "Rediscovering Lost Values," Sermon, Detroit, Michigan, February 28, 1954.
3. J. I. Packer, *Evangelical Magazine* 7, 19–20, cited in "Knowing God," 201, cited from Justin Taylor, "A Test For How Well You Understand Christianity." Blogs—October 25, 2009.

DEPART FROM ME

Benjamin Banneker a black man who invented the first Almanacs of the United States said in a letter to Thomas Jefferson, "That one Universal Father afforded us all the same sensations and endowed us all with the same faculties; and that however variable we may be in society or religion, however diversified in situation or color, we are all in the same (human) family and stand in the same relation to him"[4] It was Banneker's influence on Thomas Jefferson that caused him to write, "All men are created equal and are endowed by their Creator with certain inalienable rights and that among these are life, liberty and the pursuit of happiness."[5] One of the great American poets William Cowper puts our oneness in eloquent terms with the hope that America would cease being brutes as a nation:

> Fleecy locks and black complexion
> Cannot forfeit nature's claim.
> Skin may differ, but affection
> Dwells in black and white the same.
> Deem our nation brutes no longer,
> Till some reason ye shall find
> Worthier of regard and stronger
> Than the color of our kind.[6]

Early in our American history there were men and women who were bold enough to challenge the prevailing notion that one race is the cream of the crop. The one drop of blood theory started in America has shaped the consciousness of so many people to the point that they hide who they are so they can pass to be someone else. This sickness has destroyed lives, broken up families, caused social unrest, and brought shame to a nation that claimed to be "One nation under God, indivisible with liberty and justice for all." Faulty science and the Darwinian theory have people looking at things in racial terms when they ought to see things in human and spiritual terms. We are all humans classified as Homo sapiens. Many scientists today admit that, biologically, there is really only one race of humans.

---

4. Benjamin Banneker, "Letter to Thomas Jefferson," August 19, 1791, Africans in America, WGBH website, November 14, 2016.
5. Declaration of Independence, July 4, 1776.
6. William Cowper, "The Negro's Complaint," (1788).

Conclusion

Any true scientist will admit that the thing that sets us apart is cultural, not racial. What you find among black people, you will find among white people, among red people, among yellow people and among brown people. The same defects, deficiencies, ignorance, stupidity, selfishness, greed, and miseducation we find among white people, we find the same things among black people, brown people, red people, and yellow people. Likewise, the same intelligence, beauty, wisdom, gracefulness, and prodigy we find among white people, we also find it among black people, brown people, red people, and yellow people. Biologically, we are all the same. We all need air to breathe, food to stay alive, water to survive, and sleep to refresh ourselves. We all come from the same stock endowed with the same amenities. God is not a racist nor a nationalist or any other terms we use to divide ourselves from one another.

God didn't start this racial foolishness. God didn't start racism, sexism, or any other "ism." Humans did! It was created and put in motion by sinful humanity. America put people in racial categories to suppress them. America arrange people in hierarchies and then use religious justification to support this separation. America misguided and miseducated people. God didn't do this; America did! And, since God is not responsible for this, we cannot hold God accountable to correct it. We must correct what is wrong. We must correct the miseducation among us. We must correct man's inhumanity to man. We must stop the wars, the bloodshed, the ethnic cleaning, death and destruction as a result of racial foolishness. Unless we stop this foolishness of color prejudice and racism, pretty soon we may not have a world to live in given the power of destruction we have.

God made all people to live in this world in love, in peace, and in brotherhood. When Jesus came to earth and died for our sins, it was for the sins of the whole human race. This is why Apostle Paul said to the Galatians, "There is neither Jew nor Greek, there is neither slave nor free, there is neither male nor female; for you are all one in Christ Jesus (Galatians 3:28)." In Christ there is no distinction. There is no white, black, brown, red nor yellow. There is no American, Israeli, Palestinian, Iranian, Afghans, or any other nationality. All are one in Christ. The blood that was shed on calvary that set free the Jews from eternal damnation also set free the Gentiles, the male as well as the female. It set free all people and nationalities. From one blood, God made all people and from one blood God redeem all people through Jesus Christ our Lord. The Christianity of Christ demands that we put to rest the lie of supremacy of any race of people, and see each other as human beings endowed with the same material stuff in each of us.

Furthermore, we need to rediscover the value of love. Without love, we can never know God through Jesus Christ. It was love that brought Jesus Christ to us. John tells us, "For God so loved the world that He gave His only begotten Son, that whoever believes in Him should not perish but have everlasting life (John 3:16)." God so loved the world, not just the white world, the black, the Jew world, and the Gentile world but the whole world. Since, love is one of the Creator's major attributes, then it must be also a major attribute for His creation as well. Emphasizing how important it is for humanity to live in love, Jesus said, "You shall love the Lord your God with all your heart, with all your soul, and with all your mind. This is the first and greatest commandment. And the second is like it: You shall love your neighbor as yourself. On these two commandments hang all the Law and the Prophets (Matthew 22:37-40)." There is no question that love should be the operating principle in human relations, and when it is not we have a loveless socio-religion that is part of the ripping to pieces the social fabric of our nation. When we have a loveless religion, we allow the ugliness of life to gain a foothold in society while we ignore the devastating effects it has on society.

Jesus says to all disciples then and now, "A new commandment I give to you, that you love one another; as I have loved you, that you also love one another. By this, all will know that you are My disciples, if you have love for one another (John 13:34-35)." What does love look like? St. Augustine answers, "It has hands to help others. It has the feet to hasten to the poor and needy. It has eyes to see misery and want. It has ears to hear the signs and sorrows of [people]. That is what love looks like."[7]

Finally, to be the kind of nation we espoused to be, we must recognize the value of our need for one another. There is a genetic imperative woven within the fabric of life so we would understand our interrelatedness. God, the Great Designer of life, designed it so that we would need each other.

---

7. Augustine of Hippo, *Confessions*.

Conclusion

Regardless of race, creed, or color, we need each other. We may disagree with one another, but we need each other. We may be at different ends of the socio-economic and political spectrum, but we need each other. We may live on different sides of the track, but we need each other. Just like it takes more than one bee to make honey; just like it takes more than one contractor to build a building; just like it takes more than one fireman to put out a major fire; just like it takes more than one man to build a bridge; just like it takes more than one employee to make an automobile; it takes more than one soldier to win a war; it takes more than one Christian to advance the Kingdom of God. Each one of us is a drop in the ocean, but it takes all of us to be the ocean, an ocean of humanity working as a unified body to glorify God in a broken and fragmented world. God did not create us to be alone. God designed family; God designed community. We were not made to travel life alone; we were not made to walk alone, work alone, watch alone, wait alone, weep alone, and witness alone. "This is the interrelated structure of reality."[8] It doesn't matter if we are rich or poor, black or white, educated or uneducated, living uptown or downtown; we need each other. We did not get where we are today on our own. Somebody had to help us. Somebody had to give us a hand. Somebody gave us a chance. Somebody believed in us, and somebody sacrificed for us. Let us remember that somewhere on life's journey, we need the support of others. Show me someone self-sufficient who has never needed a helping hand, never needed encouragement, never needed advice, comfort, and direction in life, and I will show you someone totally dead. We need each other.

Moses needed Aaron; Joshua needed Caleb; Ruth needed Naomi; David needed Jonathan; Esther needed Mordecai; Mary needed Martha; Paul needed Barnabas; Abraham Lincoln needed Joshua Speed; Frederick Douglass needed William Lloyd Garrison; John F Kennedy needed Bobby Kennedy; Martin Luther King, Jr. needed Ralph Abernathy, and Jesus Christ needed his disciples. Martin Luther King, Jr. spoke about our interdependence on others. He said, "We do not finish breakfast without being dependent on more than half the world. When we arise in the morning, we go into the bathroom, where we reach for a sponge which is provided

---

8. Martin Luther King, Jr., *Strength to Love*, "The Man Who Was A Fool" (Philadelphia: Fortress Press, 1963), 70.

for us by a Pacific Islander. We reach for soap that is created for us by a Frenchman. The towel is provided by a Turk. Then, at the table, we drink coffee which is provided for us by a South American, or tea by a Chinese, or cocoa by a West African. Before we leave [our homes], we are beholden to more than half the world."[9] Christianity could be much more widespread, the church could be much more effective, and the Body of Christ could be much stronger if we would realize how much we need each other. One cannot help but agree with H. Richard Niebuhr, "Denominationalism represents the moral failure of Christianity. And unless the ethics of brotherhood can gain the victory over this divisiveness within the Body of Christ, it is useless to expect it to be victorious in the world."[10]

The Apostle Paul used our physical bodies to teach us how to work together and how each part of the body needs each other. Each member of the body has a different function, but it is still part of the one body. The whole body cannot be one member for how would the rest of the body function? Paul says, "If the whole body were an eye, where would be the hearing? If the whole body were hearing, where would be the smelling? But, now God has set the members, each one of them, in the body just as he pleased. And if they were all one member, where would the body be? But now, indeed, there are many members, yet one body. And the eye cannot say to the hand, I have no need of you, or again the head to the feet; I have no need of you (1 Corinthians 12:19-21)." Within the Body of Christ, one Christian cannot say to another Christian, I have no need of you. White Christians cannot say to Black Christians, and Black Christians cannot say to white Christians, I have no need of you. Male Christians cannot say to female Christians, nor female Christians can say to male Christians, I have no need of you. Each of us is an individual member of the Body of Christ. There is only one head to a body, and Jesus is the Head and the Chief cornerstone of the church. We are all important within the Body of Christ.

We need each other within the Body of Christ to win the world for Christ. We need each other to transform our culture. We need each other to redeem the evil times in which we live. We need each other to transform this American Christianity into the Christianity of Christ.

---

9. Ibid., 70.
10. H. Richard Niebuhr, *The Social Sources of Denominationalism*, 25.

Thomas Edison discovered the light bulb but had problems keeping the bulb lit. He tried over and over again, but he had no fix. The most he could do was keep the bulb lit for about an hour or two. People told Edison about a black man named Lewis Latimer, who discovered the filament. Latimer devised a way to help light stay lit for several hours. Edison needed Latimer's filament, and Latimer needed Edison's bulb. The white man needed the black man, and the black man needed the white man. Because they needed each other, they came together and lit up the whole world. These two people chased away the darkness of the night because they needed each other and decided to work together. If America is ever going to be a nation of freedom, justice, and democracy, then she must recognize and embrace togetherness. To get us to a more perfect union, we must rediscover lost values and move our nation from American Christianity to the Christianity of Christ.

BIBLIOGRAPHY

Books

Alighieri, Dante, *Divine Comedy*, Everybody's Library, 1995.
Bailey, E. K. And Warren W. Wiersbe, *Preaching In Black And White, What We Can Learn From Each Other*, Zondervan, Grand Rapids, Michigan, 2003.
Baldwin, Lewis V., *To Make the Wounded Whole*, Fortress Press, Minneapolis, MN, 1992.
Barclay, William, *Commentary on Matthew*, St. Andrew's Press, Scotland, 1956-1959.
Bedell, George C., Leo Sandon, Jr., Charles T. Wellborn, *Religion In America*, The Florida State University, MacMillan Publishing, New York, 1982.
Berger, Peter, *The Sacred Canopy*, Doubleday, 1969.
Blassinggames, John W., *The Frederick Douglass Paper*, Yale University Press, New Haven, CT, 1999.
Bonhoeffer, Dietrich, *The Cost of Discipleship*, MacMillan Press, 1979.
Brown, Robert McAfee, *Is Faith Obsolete*, West Minister Press, Philadelphia, PA, 1974.
———, *The Spirit of Protestantism*, Oxford University Press, New York, 1961.
Buber, Martin, *I And Thou*, T & T Clark Publishing, New York, 1937.

Bibliography

Chappell, Clovis G., *Sermons on Old and New Testament,* Harper & Row Publishers, 1953.

Cone, James H., *Black Theology & Black Power,* Orbis Books, New York, 1997.

———, *Speaking the Truth, Ecumenism, Liberation, and Black Theology,* Orbis Books, New York, 1986.

———, *A Black Theology of Liberation,* Orbis Books, New York, 1986.

Cauthen, Kenneth, *I Don't Care What The Bible Says,* Mercer University Press, Macon, Georgia, 2003.

Davis, Reginald F., *Transforming Faith To Shape The World Around Us,* Nurturing Faith, Inc., Macon, Georgia, 2019.

Douglass, Frederick, *Narrative of the Life of Frederick Douglass An American Slave,* Penguin Books, New York, 1982.

———, *The Life And Writings of Frederick Douglass, Volume 2,* Philip S. Foner, editor, International Publishers, New York, 1975.

Dunbar, Paul Lawrence, *The Complete Poems,* CreateSpace Independent, South Carolina, 2018.

Ellison, Ralph, *Invisible Man,* Vintage Books, New York, 1995.

Emerson, Michael O., Christian Smith, *Divided By Faith, Evangelical Religion And the Problem of Race in America,* Oxford University Press, Oxford, 2000.

Fosdick, Harry Emerson, *Answers to Real Problems: Harry Emerson Speaks To Our Time,* Edited by Mark E, Yurs, Wipf & Stock Publishers, Eugene Oregon, 2008.

Freire, Paulo, *Pedagogy of the Oppressed,* Continuum Publishing Company, New York, 1999.

Frost, Robert, *A Selection of Robert Frost Poems,* H. Holt and Company Publisher, New York, 1991.

Goza, Joel Edward, *America's Unholy Ghost The Racist Roots of Our Faith and Politics*, Cascade Books An Imprint of Wipf and Stock Publishers, Eugene, OR, 2019.

Hamilton, Adam, *Half Truths God Helps Those Who Help Themselves And Other Things The Bible Doesn't Say,* Abingdon Press, Nashville, Tennessee, 2015.

Hammett, Edward, H., *Making The Church Work, Converting The Church For The 21st Century*, Smyth & Helwys Publishing, Macon, Georgia, 2000.

Hugo, Victor, *Les Miserable,* 1862.

Inserra, Dean, *The Unsaved Christian Reaching Cultural Christianity with the Gospel,* Moody Publishers, Chicago, Ill., 2019.

Jones, William R., *Is God A White Racists, A Preamble to Black Theology,* Beacon Press Books, Boston, Massachusetts, 1998.

King, Martin Luther King, Jr., *A Testament of Hope The Essential Writings of Martin Luther King, Jr., edited by James Melvin Washington,* Harper & Row Publishers, San Francisco, CA, 1986.

———, *Strength To Love,* Fortress Press, Philadelphia, PA, 1963.

———, *The Radical King, Edited And Introduction by Cornel West,* Beacon Press, Boston, Massachusetts, 2015.

Kipling, Rudyard, *American Notes,* A Word to the Wise Publisher, New York, 2013.

Lewis, C. S. *Mere Christianity,* Harper One Publisher, California, 2015.

Lutzer, Erwin W., *When A Nation Forgets God,* Moody Publishers, Chicago, ILL, 2010.

MacArthur, John, *The Gospel According to Jesus, What Is Authentic Faith?* Zondervan Publisher, 1988.

Marshall, Chris, *The Little Book of Biblical Justice,* Good Books Publisher, Intercourse, PA, 2005.

Mays, Benjamin, *Quotable Quotes of Benjamin Mays,* Vantage Press, New York, 1983.

McCall, Emmanuel L., *Black Church Lifestyles, Rediscovering the Black Church Experience,* Broadman Press, Nashville, Tennessee, 1986.

Munroe, Myles, *The Burden of Freedom,* Charisma House Publisher, Lake Mary, Florida, 2000.

———, Myles Monroe, Quotes, www.goodreads.com.

Newton, Doug, *Fresh Eyes On Jesus Parables,* David Cook, Publisher, California, 2018.

Niebuhr, H. Richard, *The Social Sources of Denominationalism,* World Publishing Company, Ohio, 1929.

———, *Christ And Culture,* Harper & Row Publisher, New York, 1951.

———, *Radical Monotheism And Western Culture*, Westminster John Knox Press, Louisville, KY, 1970.

Niebuhr, Reinhold, *Moral Man and Immoral Society A Study in Ethics and Politics*, Charles Scribner's Sons, New York, 1932.

Rauschenbusch, Walter, *Christianity And The Social Crisis*, MacMillan Company, New York, 1910.

———, *Selected Writings, Edited by Winthrop S. Hudson*, Paulist Press, New York, 1984.

———, *American Reformer*, Paul M. Minus, MacMillan Publishing Company, New York, 1988.

Reich, Robert B., *The System Who Rigged It, How We Fix It*, Vintage Books, New York, 2020.

Saad, Layla, *Me And White Supremacy: Combat Racism, Change the World, And Become a Good Ancestor*, Sourcebooks, Publisher, Naperville, IL, 2020.

Sernett, Milton C., *Afro American Religious History A Documentary Witness*, Duke University Press, Durham, North Carolina, 1985.

Simon, Arthur, *Christian Faith And Public Policy No Grounds For Divorce*, William B. Eerdmans Publishing Company, Grand Rapids, Michigan, 1987.

Tillich, Paul, Love, Power, and Justice, *Christian Social Teaching, complied by George W. Corelli*, Augsburg Publishing House, Minneapolis, MN, 1966.

———, *Theology of Culture*, Oxford University Press, London, 1969.

Tisby, Jemar, *The Color of Compromise*, Zondervan, Grand Rapids, Michigan, 2019.

Thurman, Howard, *Jesus And The Disinherited*, Friends United Press, Indiana, 1981.

———, *The Mood of Christmas*, Friends United Press, Indiana, 1985.

———, *Deep River And The Negro Spirituals Speaks Of Life And Death*, Friends United Press, Indiana, 1975.

Walker, Daniel D., *The Human Problems of the Minister*, Harper & Row Publishers, New York, 1960.

Watley, William D., *Sermons on Special Days*, Judson Press, Valley Forge, PA, 1987.

Wesley, John, *The Quotable Wesley by Dave Armstrong*, Beacon Hill Press, 2014.

West, Cornel, *Prophesy Deliverance An Afro-American Revolutionary Christianity*, Westminster John Knox Press, Louisville, KY, 1982.

———, West, *Race Matters*, Vintage Books, New York, 1993.

Wilberforce, William, *Real Christianity, Revised and Updated by Bob Beltz*, Regal Publishers, Ventura, California, 2006.

Wilmore, Gayraud S., and James H. Cone, *Black Theology A Documentary History, 1966-1979, Orbis Books, Maryknoll, New York, 1979*.

———, *Black Religion And Black Radicalism*, Orbis Books, Maryknoll, New York, 1989.

Woodson, Carter G. Editor, *The Works of Francis J. Grimke*, Washington, D.C., Associated Publishers, 1942, Vol. 1, 354.

Articles

Clive Beed and Cara Beed, "Jesus On Cooperation," *Transformation*, Vol. 32, No. 2, 2015. https://journals.sagepub.com/home/trn

Fadela Chaib, "Global Hunger Continues to Rise," *World Health Organization*, 2018.

James H. Cone, "Theologians And White Supremacy: An Interview with James H. Cone," *American Magazine*, November 20, 2006.

Mark O. Hatfield, "The Sin That Scarred Our National Soul," *The Christian Century*, Vol.XC, No. 8., 1973.

William R. Jones, "Purpose And Method in Libration Theology: Implications For An Interim Assessment in Liberation Theology," 1987.

Russell D. Moore, "Can The Religious Right Be Saved?" Firstthings.com, Erasmus Lecture, January, 2017.

Rosemary Radford Ruether, "Mystification or Liberation?" *The Christian Century*, Vol. XCIV, 1977.

Charles Thomas Studd, Poetry About Jesus And Salvation, Cindy Wyatt, "Only One Life, Twill Soon Be Past," Retrieved, 2013.

Justin Taylor, "A Test For How Well You Understand Christianity." *Evangelical Magazine* 7, 19–20, October 25, 2009.

Speeches And Sermons

John Donne, *"For Whom The Bell Tolls,"* 1940.
Frederick Douglass, Speech on the "24th Anniversary of Emancipation Proclamation," Washington, D. C.,1886.
Dwight D. Eisenhower, *"The Chance for Peace,"* An address before the American Society of Newspaper Editors on April 16, 1953.
Billy Graham, "Excuses God Won't Accept," Bible Faith Mission India Ministry, Source: Decision-September, 1982.
Thomas Jefferson, Notes on the State of Virginia, Query XVIII: Manners, 1781.
Martin Luther King, Jr. *"Rediscovering Lost Values,"* Sermon, Detroit, Michigan, February 28, 1954.
———, *"Beyond Vietnam—A Time to Break Silence"* April 4, 1967, Riverside Church, New York City.
———, "The Other America," Speech given at Grosse Pointe High School on March 14, 1968.
Martin Luther King, Jr.'s last sermon, *"Drum Major Instinct,"* Ebenezer Baptist Church, February 4, 1968.
James Russell Lowell, "The Present Crisis" December 1845.
Kilroy J. Oldster, *Dead Toad Scrolls, Published by* booklocker.com, 2016. *Cited from* goodreads.com.
Martin Niemoller, *"First They Came For the Socialists,"* United States Holocaust Memorial Museum. Retrieved 5 February 2011.
Charles Spurgeon, "Almost Isn't Good Enough," www.spurgeongems.org
C.H. Spurgeon, "Preparation For Heaven" No. 3538 Sermon at Metropolitan Tabernacle Pulpit, Newington, Published on November 16, 1916, Volume 62.
Tozer Devotional/ Preparing Now for Then "The Alliance Tozer Devotional" Fri. June 05, 2020.
Elie Wiesel, Nobel Peace Prize acceptance speech on Dec. 10, 1986.

ABOUT THE AUTHOR

Reginald F. Davis is a pastor, scholar, and native of Memphis, Tennessee. He is the author of nine additional books in the field of theology and religion including *Bible Study for Busy Pastors and Ministers* and *Transforming Faith to Shape the World Around Us*. He has lectured at colleges, universities, and churches across the nation. He holds a Bachelor of Arts from Incarnate Word College, a Masters of Divinity from Colgate Rochester Divinity School, and a Ph.D. from Florida State University.

He lives in Williamsburg, Virginia, with his wife and children.

www.ingramcontent.com/pod-product-compliance
Lightning Source LLC
Chambersburg PA
CBHW010856090426
42737CB00019B/3383